Shaya

Ancestral Spirits
Awaken Me

Based on the true story of nine generations of women

Loves, Losses, and Lessons

Violet April (Shaya) Ebersole

the Peppertree Press

Sarasota, Florida

ISBN: 0-9778525-2-0
Printed in United States of America
Printed May, 2006

Acknowledgements

My research has taken me far and wide. The following organizations have helped me immeasurably.

- Monacan Indians of Virginia
- Virginia Historical Society, Richmond, Virginia
- Library of Virginia and Archives Research Services, Richmond, Virginia
- Archives and Manuscript Reading Room, Richmond, Virginia
- Chickahominy Historical Center of Charles City, Virginia
- Natural Bridge Historical Site, Virginia
- Colonial Williamsburg, Virginia
- DeWitt Wallace Decorative Arts Museum (Public Hospital Exhibition), Williamsburg, Virginia
- Amherst Library, Virginia
- Madeira, Ohio, Historical Society
- Madeira, Ohio, Library

My heartfelt appreciation to my editor, Sandy Chase, of WordMasters; my publisher, Julie Ann Howell of the Peppertree Press; and my graphic designer, Vern Firestone, Creative Director for the Peppertree Press. A special thanks to Bebe Fass Rice, author of *The Place from the Edge of the Earth*, and Milena McClain, Ph.D. I also wish to acknowledge Phyllis Cobb, 2005 Public-Relations Consultant for the Sarasota, Florida, Reading Festival.

I owe a debt of gratitude to all my family for their support and inspiration, without which I could not have realized my dream. My husband, Dick Ebersole, traveled with me from Florida to Ohio, Pennsylvania, and Virginia, wherever my search led. My mother, Violet Betty Shook, saved all the family albums and records. But more important, she gave me the gift of support and encouragement. My son, Darren, built my computer, provided me with the computer program "Family Tree Maker," and created my website, which you can reach by keying in the following address from yahoo.com: *April@aprilsweb.com*

My daughter Brandi helped me research Mary Jane Boatwright's history. My daughter Violet Eve proofread my manuscript for substance. My grandchildren, Travis, Tricia, Tiffany, Gabrielle, and Kyleigh, inspired me. Aunt Peggy helped me with researching our family's genealogy. My cousin David and his father, Robert Wick, helped gather and interpret census and family information. My grandmothers: Mary Jane, Mary Ann, Maggie, Belle, and Violet motivated me throughout my journey.

I am indebted to all of you. With you at my side, I have soared to new heights.

I thank you all sincerely.

April (Shaya) Ebersole
March 2006

Foreword

We require love and acceptance. Our nature is to find a connection to a special person or combination of people in order to enrich, enhance, and deepen our lives. My destiny was to connect with the rich past of my people, the Monacan Indians.

Two Indian ancestral spirits, my great-great-great-great grandmother and her daughter reached out to me through my dreams, sharing their life stories with me.

I have read much about dreams, especially books by Patricia Garfield, Ph.D., who states that dreams help grieving individuals find peace, enabling them to let go of deceased loved ones. But for me, my dreams are a way to help me hold onto my ancestors and ensure that they will be with me and my family forever. To preserve their stories and reclaim a culture that was taken away so many years ago, I have written *Ancestral Spirits Awaken Me*.

By breathing life into a lineage of strong, beloved matriarchs, I have been able to start anew. What a hard life, fraught with challenges and illness is now one of harmony and remarkably improved health. I believe that the connections to my past are responsible for that new life.

When I was born, my parents and I lived with my maternal grandparents on their Ohio farm until I was three. At that time my grandparents moved to Florida and my parents and I moved to a small country town in Ohio, where my dad worked in a factory and my mom took on part-time jobs, like babysitting, cutting hair for a dollar, and working in the school cafeteria in order to supplement our meager income, while caring for me and my brother.

Although life was hard, my mother always gave me what I needed—love and patience. But it was Grandma Violet who gave me gold: stories about our Indian family history that stirred my imagination. I would spend as much time as possible far out in the woods pretending that I had to survive, living there alone in a small fort that I built.

I married very young and had a son. Before I could really enjoy married life, I was plagued with debilitating arthritis, which contributed to the breakup of my short-lived marriage. Three years later my health condition improved. I remarried and gave birth to a daughter. But then I struggled with ulcerated colitis and was hospitalized several times because of severe dehydration. Four years later, pregnant, and with no one to support me, I decided to leave Ohio and move near my grandma and my parents, who had moved right next door to my grandparents in Florida.

I moved into my grandma's garage, caring for my children and working odd jobs until I gave birth to my third child four months later. I rented a small house and struggled to get by on my own with three young children. I worked many jobs, but I was always there for my children. During those years I lost many older members of my family, including my grandpa, great-aunt, and my dad from cancer, but I still had my grandma and mom, whom I visited often in the evenings.

My health problems returned, this time with a vengeance. Two years after my dad passed away, when I was 30, I had to fight cervical cancer. Two years later I was diagnosed with ovarian cancer. When I recovered, I worked at a nursing home as the full-time recreation director. Finally believing that my life was back to normal, I found two lumps in my breast, the precursor to the reappearance of cancer a few months later. At 44, facing my own mortality, I was anxious about leaving my children when they still needed me.

Energized by those thoughts, I never gave up, and my health improved through diet, exercise, and meditation, concentrating on the sounds of nature, feeling the movements of breezes, and seeing wildlife in the environment. I also gazed at the stars and moon before going to bed. In essence, I returned to a life that my ancestors enjoyed and revered.

Having lived a single life for many years, I married one of the nursing-home administrators in 2000 and quit work at his request so we could enjoy life together. In 2002 my sweet Grandma Violet passed away. But I found that she was still with me in my dreams.

Grandma Violet had told me stories about my family when I was just a child. A few years before her passing, when Grandma's memory had begun to fade, I started writing down the stories I remembered from childhood in order to preserve them. I even collected pictures, documents, and her personal items—all to aid my memory. After her passing, I realized that I could not accept life without her, so I started to search for her. I wrote notes to her, about her, and studied everything that she had done in her life.

The more involved I became in my quest, the more I started to connect to the people whom my grandma loved, including her mother Belle, her aunt Amelia, and her great-grandmother, Mary Ann, women you will be meeting shortly. These powerful women began coming to me in my dreams, sitting and talking with me in the cool, dark, misty garden.

With every dream, I felt even more compelled to search for my family history. I found peace and harmony in my connection with my ancestors. I saw how powerful these women were to survive their life trials, and I felt a growing bond. Three years passed quickly as I pursued my research in earnest, taking notes to preserve my information.

My health improved greatly as I could feel the strength of my female ancestors within me. My love for them increased the more I grew to know them. It was as if I witnessed their lives. I could smell their homes, taste their food, and sense the activities of their lives. I realized that I was experiencing their emotions, passions, and wishes.

I believe that what I have experienced might help others to look at their own lives and ancestors with different eyes. I am grateful for the opportunity to share this book and feel that it is one of my greatest accomplishments and delights. I hope it will bless your spirit and give you strength.

Table of Contents

Dedication to the Future

Travis, my first-born grandchild: Seeing you for the first time, I knew that you would be strong and peaceful. Stay strong and focused on your goals. You'll rise up to soar. Brave Eagle is your name.

Tricia, my first-born granddaughter: You have melted my heart from the first time our eyes met. You're resourceful, creative, and empathetic; you truly understand others. Put these talents to good use. You are your mother's Wenonah. Make her proud. Wolf Eyes is your name.

Tiffany: You are my gentle nature girl. You have a special loving way with people and animals. Your sense of humor often makes me laugh. You're also artistic and creative. Nurture your talents so they can continue to grow. Doe Eyes is your name.

Gabrielle: You are a strong-willed leader but also elegant. People are drawn to you, and you light up their lives. Your confidence will propel you to greatness in whatever you undertake, whether it be dancing, singing, or swimming. You are *Wechumpe*. Your name is Two Morning Stars.

Kyleigh: Learning comes naturally to you and I hope you use all your many special gifts to take wing through your life. You are indeed an artist, and you and I are both birds soaring above the trees, searching. White Dove is your name.

You all bring me such joy. And I hope that this family saga will stir some sparks in your hearts and spirits. A special place in my heart holds each one of you, as I watch you continue to thrive.

As you read about your lineage, remember how your ancestors were honest, respectful, and fair. They worked hard for their families and gave of themselves. They respected creatures and Mother Earth.

Be proud of your heritage and help it flourish. In dedicating this book to you, I hope that ancestral spirits awaken you as well.

The Dream Flight Into Yesterday

A distant spirit voice shatters the sleepy silence, sending echoes
through the hazy night.
A bird soars just above the trees searching,
as the last bits of light fade to gray.
Shadowing clouds glide by on a deep purple sky.
A small fire crackles as a woman opens her eyes.
Far off another lonely voice calls.
Steam from her breath lifts and glides away.
The cool Blue Mountain brook continues to flow over rocks to
the river.
And the stars look on in compassion.
Another day is slipping
into yesterday.
And a new generation
has arrived on Mother Earth.

Maternal Lineage:
Mary Jane Boatwright

4th Great - grandmother	Husband	Year Married	Children
Mary Jane Boatwright (1810-1844)	William Penn (circa 1805-1865)	1837	Mary Ann (1838-1924)

1
Earth-Walk (1810-1844)

Granddaughter, wake up and quietly follow me to the Whispering Garden, where I can talk to you. I am your great-great-great-great grandmother, Mary Jane. My message comes to you from across the gap of life, time, space, spirits, and shadows. I have arrived on the Wind of Peace created by your desire. I am as I was when I left my Earth-walk over 160 years ago.

First, I want you to know that you and I are one—separated by time but connected through blood. I know that you are searching for answers. I know you feel this connection, too. And I want you to share what you learn with your children and your children's children so that our story can continue forever.

I cannot hold your hand while walking through the forest, go wading with you through the cool creek water, or share food and stories by the fire. I cannot teach you my native language, songs, and traditions as I would like, but I do want you to know about my life, our family, and our people—your people, the Monacans. If you continue to listen with your heart and search for me, you will continue to learn.

Wechumpe is the name that my parents often called me. It means *like the stars*. Mother said that I was their bright and happy child. My birth name was Mary Jane Boatwright. Boatwright was our family name because my grandfather and his father built boats and canoes, which was a very important job. Many rivers, streams, and creeks ran through our land, and control of the waterways was important to our survival.

Although these waters created natural barriers, we still needed to protect our people from unfriendly tribes who lived nearby. The Cherokee lived to our west and south; the Iroquois, to the north; and the Algonquin, to the east. If we were not watchful, hostile tribes could steal our food and enslave our women and children.

A few other Boatwright families lived near us. My mother, father, and I lived in a one-room cabin next to my mother's parents. Indian men left their family when they married and became part of the wife's family. Women helped make most decisions about our people, except for the decisions made by the War Council.

We belonged to the Monacan Tribe, which was part of the Sioux Nation. *Lords of the forest* and *free spirited* were words often used to describe our people. Because everything we needed was found in the forest or rivers, our families were independent. The Sioux men were skilled in the art of hunting and fighting. Our people were skilled at making arrows, spears, and traps. But for the most part, we were farmers who wanted peace.

We believed that we were only one part of the giant creation. Respect was important in my home. We respected our elders, one another, Mother Earth, creatures, and plants. My mother taught me that beauty exists in generosity. She said that in giving a most-prized possession, I would receive the taste of happiness, and she was right.

We looked forward to gatherings and ceremonies with other Monacan people, where we would listen to the music of drums, rattles, and other instruments. I loved the dancing and sharing of food around the campfire. We always had large gatherings in the spring and during harvest time. Women would tell fascinating stories about their men stalking, hunting, and capturing every kind of game. I played and swam with the other children. We watched the men compete in contests and take part in games. My father, a strong and honest man, was one of the fastest runners.

My mother thought that I would find a husband at one of our ceremonies, but I did not think so because I always felt that there was something a little different about me. Maybe all girls think like that, but my hair just did not look as straight and shiny as most of the other girls' hair. And although I had an oval-shaped face and brown eyes like the other children, my skin color was not as dark as my friends', even though I spent most of my time outdoors.

So I would continue waiting for a sign or at least some extraordinary feeling to strike me. Then I would know the man who was meant to be my true husband. I did not worry because I had time.

My mother also told me that I was related to the old Powhatan chief, father of Pocahontas. Mother said that one of my grandmothers was born on the Chickahominy River and spoke Algonquin. Because I was the first-born daughter, I was taught that it was my responsibility to help my elders and unfortunate people. I would bring supplies and help around their homes. Mother said that I was her *Wenonah*, a daughter who makes her mother proud, just as I am proud of you, Granddaughter.

My grandmother, your 6th great-grandmother, would tell me that in olden times, our people followed and hunted the buffalo, which provided us with food, hides, and other necessities. You should have seen the beautiful blankets that we made from this animal. When we took the life of a buffalo and other animals, we gave thanks to them for sustaining us. We used every part of the animals we hunted, wasting nothing. Grandmother even used the buffalo teeth to decorate clothing, and buffalo bones to make buttons and tools. We kept Mother Earth clean and made good use of her generous gifts.

For the most part, I thought my childhood was wonderful but uneventful. My parents took good care of me and gave me much attention and love. Mother cared for me during the day. And Father spent the evenings with us after working on the boats or hunting. I enjoyed making jewelry from the beads, shells, and stones I collected from the creek, and caps from acorns I found in the forest. I strung or tied all these trinkets on long strips of leather that I cut from hides or string from the trading post. I also made small pouches to store the tools we needed for work. Mother and I wore them at our waist. I made one for father's tobacco and another for his knife.

Mother and I gardened, and I tended to the *Three Sisters*, which are the corn, beans, and squash. My mother taught me to make blankets, baskets, shoes, and clothes from plants and hides, some of which we took to the trading post, run by the White Man. These new settlers traded modern-day tools, and Grandmother especially loved her scissors, needles, knife, and cooking pots, which we received in exchange for our baskets, furs, and food.

Indian women owned their homes and everything in them. If the women divorced, the husband had to leave, and she kept the house and children. My mother taught me right from wrong. She would never allow my father to strike me. Mother said that men should show respect to women because they perform important tasks, including delivering babies and nurturing the family. She knew how to stand up for herself because her beliefs were strong and firm.

Many chores filled my day, such as gathering wood, cooking, cleaning, and fetching water from Deer Creek. I returned to my home, my strong arms carrying the filled pails. I would stop to enjoy the sights and sounds of the creek and the cool breezes that blew through the trees. Mother and I spent many happy times there.

As a child, my mother kept me very clean. I liked to play and bathe in the river. We bathed often, even in winter. She would cut my hair to my shoulders to make it easier to care for and then she would take a small amount of warm fat in her hands, rubbing her palms together until the fat was slick and shiny. She would stroke this fatty liquid through my hair till it would lie down flat. Mother made me feel beautiful.

My mother and her mother taught me many truths about Mother Earth. I learned much as we worked together and searched for herbs and medicine. Remember, Granddaughter, that all plants and creatures have names and importance. Sage keeps away illness. Sweet grass is Mother Earth's gift. Rocks have different powers and uses. Some can help make fire; other rocks bring us luck.

Colors are very important, too. Blue represents the sky and stars. Green symbolizes Mother Earth and her plants. White is for life and purity.

We also chose different creatures to represent our being. The eagle is a sign for truth. She can also represent creativity and harmony. The bear eases our emotions and helps with judgement. My symbol was the wolf, because of my strength, instincts, and powerful family connection.

My family believed that we should act with reverence in all we did. We started our day with morning prayer. We began by facing the west, then turning north, then east towards the rising sun, and bowing to the south as we ended our prayer. Now we were ready to continue our day with peace and purity in our spirit. Grandmother, Mother, and I sang songs and gave thanks throughout our days.

There is an Indian legend about our people fleeing the

enemy. Just when our people came to the edge of a cliff, with nowhere to go, they stopped to pray, some starting to sing their death songs. Suddenly a mist appeared and as it drifted away, it revealed a stone bridge that connected the cliff our people stood on with the next sheer cliff, allowing our people to cross safely and give thanks. Our enemy did not follow because they were surprised by the miracle that they had just seen. This place became our holy ground.

My parents took me to visit that special place, not far from our Lynchburg, Virginia, home, several times each year. Many other Monacan people went there to pray.

"Yes, Grandmother, I know that place. My husband and I have visited Natural Bridge, the holy ground you speak of. I was so thrilled to go there and hear the story of my ancestors told by the present-day chief."

Granddaughter, we were a happy people, with plenty of fish, deer, buffalo, and birds to eat. But our hunting grounds shrank and the White Man imposed rules on us and spread disease, like smallpox among our people.

◆◆◆◆◆◆◆ Smallpox ◆◆◆◆◆◆◆

Our people were not prepared for such a disease. Smallpox took my parents and grandparents. As soon as my parents became sick, they moved in with my grandparents, who were also ill. Mother told me that I was their future and that she did not want me to get the sickness, so I stayed alone in our home, which was close to my grandparents' cabin.

The first night my parents were living with my grandparents, I was awakened by a noise and looked outside to see my father in the moonlight. He was burning cedar and sage and he splashed water onto hot rocks to create steam. I thought I heard

6

him say the word *Tunkan*, which means *rock*, and then he raised his hands to the stars.

Granddaughter, he knew that it would not be long until their Blue-spirit walk would begin. I quietly went back to my bed. That was the last time that I saw him or heard his deep voice.

My parents and grandparents suffered with the sickness. I sometimes heard them vomiting when I brought supplies to their door. Other times I heard moaning. I brought firewood, fresh water, and food to their door, but they would not let me in. Mother would talk to me at the open doorway, but she would not let me get too close to the cabin.

After a few days, I could see that they developed rashes on their mouths. And Mother's rash spread over her face, arms, hands, and legs. She told me to gather wood to start a large fire close to the cabin and place her two large cooking pans there filled with water. Late that night while I was sleeping, she washed, boiled, or burned everything they had used in order to protect me. She told me not to keep a lock of her hair when she passed, the usual custom, because she was worried that this new disease might spread to me if I kept anything of hers.

The next day Mother's fever started to fall and her face did not look as red. I thought that she was getting better, but within a short time her rash rose into bumps that filled with fluid. The fever returned, and scabs formed where the bumps had been and then fell off. I was so upset and wanted to do more to help my family, but Mother reminded me again not to come close. She made me promise.

Mother told me how much she loved me and how much happiness I had brought to her life. My family did not fear death, and they believed that after death the spirit is free to be everywhere. Mother told me how sad it would be to leave me, but she said that she believed that she would still be able to hear my prayers. She told me to remember all that she had taught me and to go to my Uncle Jim if I needed him.

After a while, the moaning got softer and then it stopped, and Mother did not come to the door to talk to me anymore. I begged her to answer my calls, but she did not come to the door. I waited two more days and then went inside to see all four of them lying there together in bundles. I could tell that my mother was the last one to go. She held out to care for the others.

I could see that she had taken four of her blankets and wrapped my father and her parents inside each one of the three blankets, saving one for herself. She sewed the outer edges, closing the blankets. Then she sewed two sides of her blanket and crawled inside, leaving the top opened.

I wondered where Mother found the strength to care for the others, even though she, too, was ready to pass on. It must have been her strong determination to protect me so that I would not have to care for my family, exposing myself to their sickness. Her love for me was stronger than her weakness and pain. I was the only one left, and I could not believe that this tragedy had happened to my family. How could they have been taken from me? I loved and missed them with all my heart.

I wrapped them carefully in animal skins, prepared food, adding needed items for the other world, and then went to Uncle Jim for help. I buried my parents in the sacred mound near the foot of Blue Mountain. Returning to my home alone, I used a knife to cut off my two braids to my shoulders to show my sadness. I did not eat for several days. And I did not care for myself. I cried for many days as I lay in the dark in my parents' cabin.

I felt that I should burn my grandparents' little cabin. So I gathered some hot coals from a fire I built and put them inside the doorway. The flames reached high into the sky, and smoke drifted off towards the mountain. Living near the mountain, I could hear the distant cry of wolves in the evening, reminding me of my loneliness.

I wondered whether my family were watching me and knew my pain. I wanted to hear their kind voices and see their cheerful faces. I wanted my mother to tell me what to do next, but her voice was silent and her face was only a beautiful memory. Often I visited the burial mound to pray in hopes that they were listening.

I was 18 summers old when my parents passed, and it was hard for me to go on at first, but I realized that I could survive. When I realized that I had to move on, I went down to the river, jumped in, and washed myself, and started planning my new life of living alone.

I knew how to harvest and make beautiful baskets for trade. I would have to go on. It was what Mother wanted when she said that I was their future. It was good to have my work and it was a comfort to look out every day to the long ridge of Blue Mountain, rising up into the sky. I pictured my family there. They would want me to be with them someday, but not yet.

Mother had chosen the spot where we had built our home. She loved the mountains. A feeling of peace would take me back to happier days and give me hope for my future. Mother used to look out to the mountain, as she made her baskets. She looked as though she was watching for someone to come for a visit or maybe she heard a voice calling her. Often, when I would call to her, she would not hear me and I would have to call to her twice before she would give me her full attention.

Granddaughter, maybe you were the one Mother was watching for because you are the one who returned.

◆◆◆◆◆◆◆ Changes ◆◆◆◆◆◆◆

Many different people had come through our land looking for riches. In 1728 peaceful surveyors traveled across the country to map out the land. But it was the settlers who came after them who hurt us. They killed our animals and burned our harvest fields, leaving us without food. They wanted everything that we had and were willing to get it in whatever way they could.

By the time I was born, many changes had occurred for my people. A few White Men had served as the big White Chief. In fact, the third one was White Chief Thomas Jefferson, who built a home near our land. My parents and I went to see his great house. Granddaughter, I had never seen such a strange-looking home. I heard other Indians talking about how Jefferson had purchased huge lands that almost doubled the size of what they called *America*. He had also sent Lewis and Clark on their famous expedition five years before I was born. The Indians talked about Sacagawea, a Shoshone girl. If not for her wisdom, the White Men would not have succeeded.

Another change was about to happen as well. With the passing of my parents, my nights, especially, were long, lonely, and too quiet. I wished for a family of my own.

There was a man in town that I had my eye on. I did not know why I was so drawn to him, and yet at the same time, I was afraid to talk to him or even look directly at him. I thought to myself that this confusing, extraordinary feeling must be what I had been waiting for. Maybe part of it was his shiny hair, big hands, and wide shoulders. He had deep, dark eyes that frightened me a little and a smile that made me want to reach out to touch his lips with my fingertips.

I could not stop thinking about him. His name was William Penn and he worked with my Uncle Jim. They were building a bridge over a branch of the Monacan River, when I first noticed William and heard Uncle call out his name. When I saw William that first time, I just watched for a few minutes and went home without even talking to my uncle. I started making more trips, passing where they worked in order to see what they were doing and catch a glimpse of William.

On one of my trips to the trading post I stopped by to see how my Uncle Jim and his family were doing because Uncle had not come by my home for a while. He said that he had just been busy working.

As I was about to leave, I was startled to see William standing behind me. I dropped my armful of baskets into the water. He ran along the river's edge and when he was ahead of the baskets, he dove into the swiftly moving water. The current brought the baskets to him. Grabbing them, he carried them to me, water dripping where he stood. His skin and black hair gleamed in the sunlight. I thanked him and gave him a basket to take home. I said that he could give it to his wife. He said that he would like to do that, but he did not have one.

When he asked me what else I could make, I told him that I made my own clothes and shoes and wove blankets. He told me that he needed a blanket, asking me how much it would cost. After that day we started spending time together.

We went for many long walks through the forest. William and I also played games. Once he heard me singing, as I was walking through the woods to meet him. He was careful not to make a sound as he followed my voice, walking in my direction. At first I did not know that he was even there until he carelessly stepped on a downed branch, making a brittle, crackling sound. I stopped singing and hid behind a tree. He sat and waited, not knowing where I was. I kept still, not wanting to give my hiding place away and let him win this game. I knew that he was eager to see me and

11

would not wait for long. Finally he said that he gave up and asked me to come out wherever I was.

I laughed at him for losing the game, giving him a pitiful face, so he chased me until he overtook me and rolled with me across the ground until I told him that he won. He kissed me and asked why I had not sung for him before. I told him that this was the first time that I had sung since my mother's Blue-spirit walk. He said that he loved my singing; it was another way to keep a part of Mother with me. After that day I sang for him often.

Then I touched a small scar near the outside corner of his right eye. I asked how he got it. He told me it was a childhood accident. He and his friend were practicing with their bows and arrows when the friend slipped on a rock. The arrow accidentally hit William in the face.

William reached out and touched my hair that hung in two braids. He pulled loose the leather strips and let my hair fall. Then he spread it over my shoulders and some fell draping across my back. He looked into my brown eyes and told me that I was beautiful.

We found a special place that we liked to go. It was high on a cliff where we could look down to see the Monacan River. On the edge of the cliff, surrounded by large rocks, was a cave in which we would sit in for hours. I would lay my head against his chest where I could hear his heartbeat. It did not take long for me to know that I loved this man. I knew that he loved me too: I could see it in his face and feel it in my heart.

Sometimes he built a small fire and we would snuggle close inside, watching the busy creatures of the woods. He and I talked; other times we just enjoyed the quiet. He told me that he loved my smile, although I thought it was a little crooked, tilting higher on the right side. Sometimes I would sing and dance. He liked when I danced because it reminded him of orange leaves falling or a feather in the wind or warm rain on the river.

The thick leaves on nearby trees also protected us from the wind. But with the changing colors of the season, the leaves started falling, and the cold wind blew harder. Even so, we would sit in our cave. His strong, tender arms would pull me close, and I could feel the muscles in his young healthy body. He would open his coat of soft fur and invite me inside. He would also bring along the blanket I made for him and wrap it around our shoulders. My body would tingle when I felt his warm skin against mine.

When the snows stopped and buds started to appear, we returned to that happy place. While sitting there, I thought that these were the best days of my life. My health was good and my spirit, overflowing with joy. My heart was my best possession, and I gave it away only when I was sure I would receive a great love in return.

William and I married in early spring. The ceremony was simple, but I can still remember our promise:

My William, as I stand beside you today, I will stand beside you through my years. I will love and care for you. I will hold you close through rain and shine. Your love came to me like a bright star on a stormy night. I will give you all I can to warm and brighten your days. Your irresistible charm blew away my misty clouds of loneliness. My love will not age or fade. I believe in you. Your soft whispers in the dark give me strength and hope. You made my dreams come alive. I love you and thank you for loving me. Today I take you to be husband. I have already given you my heart.

Granddaughter I can still remember what he promised me, as if he were standing next to me right now:

Mary, you came into my heart with softness. You are as tender as the fluff of a dandelion at the end of summer. You slipped softly into my heart as a cloud floats across the blue sky. The light of your love shines on my path like the sun and makes my spirit soar like an eagle. My life is changed because of you forever. My heart is filled with much happiness. All of my body is alive in your presence. My promise to you is to keep my heart open to join you, spirit to spirit, to stand by you, and love you all my days. I take you to be my wife. I have already given you my heart.

After our promises, he moved into my home. I no longer wore my long hair in two braids but rather in a single one down my back to show I was married. The one braid also made it easier when I did my work. In the evenings I let my hair down for my husband. William kept his hair cut short on his arrow pull-side so it would not be in his way while hunting. He also wore a shell necklace and a claw from a bear that he had killed a few years earlier during the full cold moon.

During the winter, we had a baby girl, and we named her Mary Ann. Because William called me Mary, we called our baby by her middle name, Ann. I loved them both and was happy to have a family again.

My daughter was not very old when I became sick, and I knew she would have to depend on her father for survival. There was so much that I wanted to teach and show her, as my mother had done with me, but Ann was so young. Before I took my Blue-spirit walk, Ann had just lost her first baby tooth, which I kept in a tiny pouch that I hung from a string around my neck so it would be close to my heart. I worried that she would not remember my love; I had only five summers with her. Granddaughter, I am still wearing that tooth in this pouch; I will never forget my Ann.

I wanted her to know that there is a Supreme Creator, that our people have strict rules to follow, and that those who fail to listen are punished. I wanted to teach her that there are different clans within the Monacan people and that children can trace their lineage through their mother.

Monacan women marry Indians from outside their clan to keep their children's blood rich. The husband from outside the wife's bloodline then becomes a part of the woman's clan. Marriage within a clan is severely punished and considered incest because men and women in the clan are too closely related.

How could I teach Ann all about the Monacan people in such a short time? I asked William to tell Ann about our family and home when she grew older. I wanted him to tell her about my parents, but he had not even known them. There are some things that a daughter should learn from being with her mother. I prayed with all my heart that Ann would find wisdom, happiness, comfort, health, and love in her life. There was nothing more that I could do.

◆◆◆◆◆◆◆ Mary Jane's Legacy ◆◆◆◆◆◆◆

Now, for you, my Granddaughter, I am so glad that you have shown such an interest in my life. I hope that you have found answers, and maybe they will help you to better understand yourself. I want you to know that a part of me continues through you and because of you. I hope good things for your journey on Mother Earth before your Blue-spirit walk. Be strong but gentle. Know that you are never alone. If you need me, just close your eyes and look deep inside yourself. I will always be there with you. We are one.

I believe that part of what a daughter thinks she can do is directly related to what her mother thinks or other women in her family think she can do. Granddaughter, you can do anything that you really put your mind to. I believe in you.

There is a reason for your life. Pay attention to the wind, clouds, creatures, and nature. The sun, stars, moon, and Mother Earth have natural cycles, seasons, and rhythm.

Life revolves around them. Discover the path of your destiny. Listen to your heart and spirit. There are unseen powers in the Universe. Mother Earth knows how to heal herself, but some men try to destroy her. Your own body knows how to heal if you allow it to happen. Always give thanks for the gifts that you receive. Know that I love you. Together we are the past, present, and future. I wish for your dreams to come true. Now I must leave you.

Maternal Lineage:
Mary Ann Penn's Childhood
on Virginia Farm

3rd Great - grandmother	Mary Ann's Father	Freed Slave Women	Freed Slave Women's Children
Mary Ann Penn (1838-1924)	*William Penn (circa 1805-1865)	Ellen	Arthur Elya Delaware Susan Sarah Ann
		Willie	Scott Simeon

*William Penn may have fathered Willie's children, but there are no conclusive records.

2

The Accident (1844-1852)

"As morning approaches, the time of dreaming draws to a close and visiting spirits must part. My 4th great-grandmother did not call to me again. But the next night, her daughter came to me."

Granddaughter, can you hear me? I am your 3rd great-grandmother, Mary Ann. I come to you from a great gap in time. I passed on over 80 years ago. I know that you still have many questions, so I will try to answer them for you. I know that you have not given up your searching. In your dreams you can search past the moon to find me among the stars. I will tell you about my life and my children. In my Blue-spirit walk, I can hear and you will be able to understand my speech clearly. But I am getting ahead of myself.

Come and sit here next to me. I am glad to look upon your face and see your warm smile. Your face is like a mirror, reflecting my high cheekbones and oval face of my youth. You have my daughter's green eyes and dark-brown hair.

Your strong drive to connect with your ancestors proves your determination and sincerity. You have searched for me, not with just curiosity and interest but with a desire to know, a truthful heart, and an open spirit to learn. I do not tell you this story for you to feel sorry for me but rather for you to understand and know me. You will, without a doubt, be very much surprised by what you learn as I share my life story with you, but no more so than I was as the seasons changed and events unfolded.

We all go through a similar journey in our Life-walk. All people have needs of their body, mind, and spirit. We all face trials and then find different ways to handle our situations. The results make up our life story. Our individual wisdom, strength, attitudes, and decisions play a big part in this outcome.

This world was rapidly changing and for me it was full of love, loss, and tragedy. I saw five generations of our family in my 85 years, though my mother was not with me for long. She feared that I would not remember much about her, but I want you to know that I did.

◆◆◆◆◆◆◆ Mother's Song ◆◆◆◆◆◆◆

I remember her arms tenderly holding me as I would go to sleep at night and I can still feel the soft, comforting warmth of her blanket as she placed it around me, keeping out the night chill. As she bent down to kiss me, her long, dark hair smelled like a fresh summer rain in the meadow. The smooth strands of her braid felt like silky threads. I can hear in my head the melody of her sweet, loving voice as she spoke and sang to me. Mostly, I remember feeling safe and secure when she was near, followed by great pain when she left me.

I even faintly remember some words to a song Mother sang, though I do not know the full meaning or the exact words. I will sing it to you now.

Oh Ho Oh Ho Shaya holta—Heya Heya Monticoma—No Guy Holta Neah—Lopeach u Now Away—Lopeach u Now Away. Stars shine from up above—Leading my way to see—my spirit like a dove.—I have found—My destiny—Found—My destiny.

December 5, 1838 was the date of my birth in our small Virginia cabin. My father said that a strong cold wind was blowing outside on that wintry night, but I was kept warm in Mother's arms while she sat next to the fire, singing songs of happiness and thanksgiving for my new life. She gave thanks to the Great Spirit of the East for her strength—to the South for her warm spirit—to the West for harmony—to the North for self-control—to Heaven for the ancestors—to Mother Earth for fruitfulness—to her Soul within for her fulfilled desires.

She was a loving mother and wife, who wanted everything good for our family. Father would describe her to me often so I would not forget what she looked like. He would tell me that I looked like her. She was a little bit more than 5 feet of beauty and grace. Her face was smooth and youthful. Strong and thin, she worked hard raising me and taking care of Father.

Father said that Mother loved me with a heart as big as Blue Mountain near our home. She always wanted to be there for me, to help and teach me, but she could not stay because she became sick. She hated to leave me and prayed for her strength to stay, but it did not come to her, not even for one more day of life.

◆◆◆◆◆◆◆ Severed Roots ◆◆◆◆◆◆◆

I loved my Lynchburg home, where I could still feel the presence of Mother, even though she had been gone for three years. But we had to leave quickly because we were having trouble with some of the nearby settlers. Two of Father's close Monacan friends had gone out hunting and never returned home. Some farm animals were also missing. We heard how the White Man was threatening our people and treating Indians cruelly. The White Man forced us to move. Father was a brave man, but he

21

promised Mother he would care for me. He was worried about my well-being if something happened to him, so he told me that we must go.

Father took me away late one night, leaving most of our things behind. As we traveled, I thought that I would never forgive Father for forgetting my doll and blanket that Mother made for me for my fifth birthday just before she passed over. He left her beautiful baskets just sitting in the corner of the room next to her beaded moccasins.

We were traveling by foot, so we could take only what he could carry. Father also knew that he would have to carry me, especially across the swift waters and up the steep mountains, so he could take only necessary supplies like a few weapons, some tools, and a coat and blanket for us.

As I was being carried away, I could hear the howling of a lone wolf on the side of Blue Mountain. I felt that she was telling me good-bye. I raised my head, blinked my sleepy eyes, and lifted my hand in her direction. I strained to listen as we walked farther away from the sad sounds. I felt that the hours and days took me farther away from the comfort of my memories of Mother.

As we traveled north by northeast, Father was busy finding food and shelter for us. We mostly traveled in the safety of the dark night, because Father did not want anyone to see us.

The White Man was always on the watch for runaway slaves and Indians, who were sometimes taken away to be used as slave labor. Many White Men hated Indians as much as they hated Negroes. The White Man wanted to wipe out the Indian race for the rich hunting grounds. White Men said things like, 'There are no good Indians. You cannot trust an Indian. We need to move the savages all out west.' White Men called Indian women and children terrible names. Negroes and Indians needed traveling papers. Without warning, they could be shot, whipped, or attacked by dogs. Granddaughter, these were dangerous times.

During our travels, we would stop at the homes of a few Monacan Indians, who gave us food and a place to sleep. Their way of life was also falling apart around them as were the lives of other Indian tribes. The White Man started giving English names to our land and waterways. Many Cherokee Indians were being pushed west, herded like cattle and dying along the way. The White Man was purposely spreading disease by giving Indians infected blankets at the trading posts. Many Indians were finding it harder to protect their families against the increasing numbers of White Men.

Early one starry morning, as we were just about to drift off to sleep, we heard footsteps coming through the darkness. With my eyes I told Father not to leave me, but he put his coat over me and slipped away. I shivered silently at the base of a large oak that had a few broken low-hanging branches, fearing that I would lose him, too. I spoke to my mother in my spirit voice and asked her to come and take me away to be with her. She did not answer.

Minutes later, I heard the quiet, frightened voices of two women talking to my father. I peeked out from under the coat as I heard them walking towards me. The three of them were not alone. They were closely followed by a few small figures. As they arrived at the tree, Father whispered for me to come out. The women and their children were Negroes also headed north. They told Father they were free because their owner had promised his wife on her deathbed that he would free her personal slaves.

The frightened women were unsure of their destination, so they were glad to meet up with us. Father told me that they would be traveling with us to the home of some of our relatives in Fauquier County, also in Virginia.

At first, I was not very happy to have them join us. Father meant everything to me. I had no one else since Mother's passing, and I was afraid that these strangers would take him away from me. I was not sure whether I could still be the center of Father's attention with so much else going on. Father was mine and I did not want to share him. But by the next morning, I could see that it might be fun to have other children around.

I learned that the two women's names were Ellen and Willie. Ellen was Father's age and Willie was younger and very pretty. All the children belonged to Ellen. Arthur was the oldest boy. He was nine, a little older than me but about my same height. Elya was five; Delaware, four; and Baby Susan, two. I had not seen the baby that first night because she was wrapped in a blanket, fast asleep, hanging on her mother's back. As I watched Ellen carry her baby the next day, I thought of my mother and how much I wanted to be with her again. I caught Father's eye watching me, as I looked at them and knew that he knew my thoughts.

We rested for that day and started on our journey again at nightfall. We arrived at our destination a few days later. All of us stayed with an older couple at a rundown, old farm. Father called the couple Uncle Will and Aunt Lizzy.

Aunt and Uncle were surprised to see all of us, especially Willie, Ellen, and all her children. But Father told Uncle Will and Aunt Lizzy that extra people could help around the farm. Aunt and Uncle felt happy and excited for the help because they were growing older and having much trouble keeping up the farm.

Uncle Will explained that the farm was falling apart. The roof leaked. A hinge on the front door was missing, so it had to be lifted and dragged to shut it. A few boards were missing or broken on the house and front porch. The garden had more weeds than vegetables. The barn was dirty and the pigs had escaped through the broken-down fence. Chickens were laying their eggs in unknown places.

We each had jobs to do in exchange for our keep. We

worked very hard, starting early each morning, to try to get the farm back in shape.

A man who knew Father helped him find a job as a stone-mason. I had overheard Father tell Uncle, 'I can do the work because I learned these skills as a boy when I helped build a mission near my home.' The time was right for Father because many buildings were being built, and strong, skilled masons like Father were valued.

Ellen and Willie were accustomed to working hard and were happy to be living as free women with their children. Aunt Lizzy cooked and Uncle Will told us stories and sang funny songs in the evenings by the fire. We did not take long to fall asleep once we climbed up into the loft and crawled into our beds. Willie, Elya, and I slept up there together where the air was warmed from the heat of the fire. Sleeping on the pile of bedding, I felt like a bird nesting in a tree. Father and Arthur slept outside. But when it was cold or wet, they slept in the barn.

When I was young, I often dreamt of running away to my childhood home to rescue something to remind me of Mother. All that I had were Father's stories and a feeling in my heart. But I wanted her to hold me again. I cannot remember how old I was, maybe 11 or 12, when I decided that the only way to hold onto my mother was to take her name, so I called myself Mary Ann. Father was glad when I asked him to call me Mary Ann instead of just Ann.

A few months after we arrived at the farm, Uncle Will passed away on a steamy hot afternoon. Uncle had been working in the field when Arthur found him. Uncle's legs were spread on the ground and both his hands were opened over his heart. He was staring wide eyed into the bright sun. His face and mouth tried to yell, but nothing could be heard except for Arthur's scream. We all came running, expecting to see a big snake or something that might be fun. Then we saw Uncle Will lying there between rows of vegetables.

It was hard for Arthur to sleep for a while after that day. Ellen told us that finding Uncle Will must have reminded Arthur of his father's murder by the overseer just days before they had started on their journey north. Arthur actually saw his father being murdered. Father gave me one of his looks that told me not to ask for any details. So I never knew more about that story.

Aunt Lizzy was so sad about Uncle's death that she just wanted to move to Cincinnati, Ohio, to be with her sister Margaret, who had moved there years earlier. Lizzy sold the farm to us, and Father gave her all the money he had saved from his first few months at his job. He was saving every penny so he could buy a place anyway. Aunt Lizzy had plenty of money for her trip and even some left over. Father said that he would send her more money later when he earned more. He did not like being in debt.

A couple of weeks after we buried Uncle Will, Aunt Lizzy packed some bags and rode off, wearing her best bonnet and dress. She rode down our dusty path in a small, black jiggling carriage drawn by a silver horse with a long black tail and mane. She had been so nice to me and now she was leaving. I watched as the carriage grew smaller and smaller and then disappeared around a bend covered with tall grasses.

I closed my eyes quickly, held my breath, and wished that she might change her mind and return. But when I opened my eyes, she was still gone. As the dust settled, I noticed the sounds of the crickets. Their screeching started to sound as though they were laughing at me. Once again someone had left me. My body started to tighten and I squeezed my fists. Running, through the field far away from the house, I cried, 'Come back to me!'

I became aware that I was not just talking to my aunt. I was also talking to my beloved mother. I dropped down to the ground and started crying. Memories of Mother's tenderness flowed into my mind. I remembered a game that Mother taught me to help me go to sleep at night. She told me to close my eyes, think of beautiful things that I loved, and remember as many details as I could. I would then whisper those details to Mother and fall asleep. As I lay in the field, alone with my thoughts and memories, I forced myself to think about the things that I loved, like the laughing babbling book, songbirds, and the feel, smell, and sounds of dancing winds and Mother's singing.

I was surprised early the next spring when Ellen had a baby girl. I woke up one morning before the sun came up to hear Ellen's moaning. Father had gone on his way to work, and everyone else was sleeping. It scared me at first because I thought Ellen was hurt or dying. I woke Willie so she could help her. To my surprise, it was not an end of life but a beginning.

Ellen told me that she named her baby Sarah and asked me whether it was okay if the baby could be called Sarah Ann. Ellen wanted to use my middle name. Of course, I said 'Yes!' It made me feel proud. That was my happiest day since Mother left.

Ellen had never said one word about expecting a baby. I wondered whether she knew that it was going to happen or whether she was surprised, too. I thought she must have been surprised because how could anyone keep something like that a secret?

Sarah Ann was very loud and demanding. For the first few months she was quiet only when she was dry, with her belly full, or when she was sleeping. She had to be changed often and she woke everyone at night, but we all enjoyed her funny faces, squeaky noises, and awkward movements as she grew.

As if Baby Sarah Ann was not surprise enough, a few months later Willie also had a baby, but he was a boy named Scott. Father appeared to be very happy to have another boy in the house. Father also praised me for helping with the little ones, making me want to help that much more.

Elya was the hardest one of the children to get along with. She was usually my helper, but she did not like helping me or doing any chores. Elya would not even listen to her mother. Often I helped Elya with her work just to get it done before Father came home so I could please him. Elya learned to take advantage of me, and, in time, I found myself doing double-work. Even though I told myself that it was my fault, I did not know how to stop.

When Scott and Sarah Ann were about three years old, Willie had another baby boy, and she named him Simeon Penn. Again Father was glad to see another little boy. It was 1849 and I was 11 years old. This time I noticed that Willie's body had grown larger before she had her baby. I had not noticed it when the other babies were born because I was too young to understand. The big aprons that Ellen and Willie wore over their dresses also covered their shapes.

A few times when I tried to question Father about Ellen and Willie, he made it clear to me that it was not my place to ask questions about adults, so I accepted his guidance. Father could have asked one of the women in the house to explain these things to me, but he never did. Anyway, having babies was a private, secretive matter. It was almost like a mystery. I longed for my mother, and as time passed, Father talked less and less to me about her, but I still thought of her every day.

We had a house full of adults and children, and we were always busy. Clothes had to be washed; babies, cared for; and food, prepared. Arthur cut wood for fires, and Delaware stacked the cut wood and brought some into the house for cooking and heating. Susan scared birds from the garden, while she picked out bugs and weeds. She also found eggs and small turtles for soup. Ellen and Willie made our clothes, cooked, cleaned, and gardened.

Elya and I plucked feathers and saved them for bed stuffing. Willie taught us to darn. Many of our jobs changed with the seasons. We had times to plow, plant, weed, and harvest.

We did not go to school. So I did not learn to read or write. Ellen and Willie did not know how to read either, so they could not teach us. There was too much work to be done to worry about school anyway. At least Father had taught me about numbers and money. He gave me lessons during the winter months when we did not have as much work to do. He said that I would have a need in the future to know about money. I enjoyed learning from him and receiving extra attention.

During my 12th summer I started to have my first moon time. For a few days, I noticed a stain on my underdrawers when I bathed and washed my clothes. Then I saw a little blood that really worried me. I wondered whether I was going to have a baby or maybe I was going to die. By the next day, I knew that I had to talk with someone. Finally I went to Ellen, when I saw her outside alone. She told me it was a natural time of growing when a girl starts changing into a woman. She said that all women have this in common whether they are Indian, Negro, or White.

Ellen told me that she would make a special dinner, which would be our secret celebration of my changing. She let me sit in her chair at the table instead of sitting on one of the long, crowded benches that Father had made for the children. She served me my food right after serving Father. I did not have to wait for all the little ones. Best of all, I did not have to help with the dishes. She looked across the table at me, smiled, and we knew that we were connected because of our secret.

Father tried to ask Ellen about the change in our routine, but Ellen looked at him, shaking her head and tightening her lips to let him know not to ask. I was surprised because I had never seen that side of her before. Father was a little surprised, too, but he must have decided that she had her reasons. So he continued talking about his plans for the farm. I wished that I could have shared this evening with my mother, but I was very glad to have Ellen to talk to.

I wondered whether Father had noticed that I had changed, but I did not say anything to him about it. Over the next year I began looking more like a woman, and there was no way that he could have missed those changes. He said, 'Mary Ann, you look more like Mother every day.' My heart swelled with love for my father and my dear mother. From then on everyone called me Mary Ann, and Mother was with me forever.

Summer came again, and one day when Elya and I were out picking plump, dark berries while watching the three little ones, she took off, leaving me alone with the children. She had placed only a few berries in the bottom of her pan before slipping off. I called and called her name but she did not come back to help.

We were not aware that Father was on his way home at that same time I was looking for Elya: He had just lost his job because he was accused of stealing from Dudley Smith's General Store. Mr. Smith hated Indians, and he told everyone that the town would be better off without them because they could not be trusted. He felt that we were taking away jobs from the White Man.

He saw his chance to get rid of another Indian when he saw Father walking toward the store. Mr. Smith falsely accused Father of stealing from the store and persuaded Father's boss to fire Father and withhold his pay. Because most White Men watched out for one another, Father's boss agreed with Mr. Smith and fired Father on the spot. My father was not even allowed to defend himself.

Father had no money to bring home for his week of hard

labor. Having no job to return to distressed and confused him. There were 11 of us to care for, and we still owed money for the farm.

We were all doing our chores, except for Elya, who was swinging on a vine that hung from her favorite tree on the other side of our hill. Ellen, Susan, and Willie were weeding the garden. Arthur was busy chopping wood as Delaware stacked. I was watching the younger children.

When Father saw what Elya was doing, he became angry. He had warned her time after time that she had to contribute and not leave all the work for me. I looked out and saw that Father's jaw was clenched and his lips, squeezed so hard that his chin was turning red. His eyes had a shrunken glare, with his eyebrows lowered and his forehead wrinkled.

As he rode his old mare across the field, I saw a whip in his hand and knew that he was going for Elya. I yelled to Sarah Ann not to let go of Simeon's hand, and I started running as fast as I could to stop Father. The little ones were trying to catch up to me.

Father yelled at Elya, as he snapped his whip in the air next to her and pulled back his strong arm to strike again, just as I came running up closer to stop him. I was not sure whether he was going to hit her because he had never done it before. He did not see me as he threw out his arm and his whip whirled through the air and wrapped around my head.

Father dropped the whip, jumped down from his horse, and ran to me. As he unwrapped his whip from around my eyes and ears, his hands were shaking. I could not even open my eyelids. All went dark as I wondered what could have happened to me. Then the pain set in and I could feel blood dripping down through the front of my dress and through my hair, down my neck.

I felt like cuts from sharp icicles were tearing through my flesh. It was hot and cold at the same time. I was so scared that I wanted to jump out of myself, but I did not know how to get away from the pain. Chill bumps rose on my skin and down my spine, and I drew my shoulders up. Heat washed over my face, my ears burned like fire, and my hands and underarms started to sweat. I also felt a knot in my stomach and my shaking knees, but the burning in my face and ears was all I could think about.

Father picked me up and carried me into the house. I could feel his heart pounding against my arm. Ellen and Willie wanted to care for me, but they were not sure what to do. They had never seen a wound like this; there was much swelling. The next day a sticky, warm liquid started to drip from my wound. I was so scared and worried that I stopped talking. I could not see and I worried that I might never see again. I could barely hear in one ear. All I heard was humming, like a bee buzzing in my ear, and I wanted to stop that noise.

Willie went for our neighbor, Ann Thompson, who took her carriage to look for her friend, Doc Gooding. We had never had him come to our house or even care for any of us before, but we all knew of him and I had seen him once when Father and I had gone into town for some supplies. The doctor's office was near the general store. And I remember asking Father who was the tall, thin man with the long white beard? And why was he carrying a small black bag?

Doc Gooding came to the house to see my injury. I strained to hear as he told father that I would go blind or deaf or maybe both. He told father to take me to the hospital in Williamsburg. There was a doctor there who was doing wonders with patients, some who suffered head injuries. Maybe he could help me.

3
The Insane Asylum
(1852-1862)

It did not take long for me to realize that this hospital was a dreadful, frightening place. Doctor Galt, the specialist recommended by Doc Gooding, took time examining me and listening to Father's account of the horrible incident. I squeezed Father's hand as the doctor lifted my chin and moved my head from side to side.

Doctor Galt accepted me as a patient, and Father had to leave, saying his final good-bye as he wrapped his large arms around me, kissed my forehead, and then slipped away. I reached out to touch him, but he was no longer close to me. I was so upset that I crossed my arms and did not say a word. I could not believe that he was really going to leave without me. I had not even said good-bye.

For a long time after his farewell, I wanted to tell Father that I forgave him for leaving my doll and blanket in Lynchburg and I forgave him for the accident. I would forgive him for leaving me here alone if he would just come back and take me away with him. He did not come back, just like Mother and Aunt Lizzy. I started to think less about Father as time went by and the swelling around my eyes disappeared.

I was so excited one spring morning as I awoke. My sense of smell seemed to have grown stronger to make up for my not being able to hear well. Now I could smell the blossoms of the fruit trees carried on the breeze. Even though the window in my room was rarely opened, I could still smell the sweet fruit, which helped to mask the strong odors of the asylum. I never got used to the smells of stale urine from the chamber pots mixing with the foul odors of residents' bodies and musty bedding.

I turned toward the sweet fruit smell and stretched my fists and arms above my head. Suddenly I realized that I could also see flashes of light instead of the darkness I had come to know. I could actually see sunlight in my room. I stood there not knowing what to do, but I was so thrilled that I allowed myself to laugh. I had to turn away from the window because my eyes were starting to hurt.

As time went on, I was able to see movement and then shapes; my vision continued to improve. I decided not to tell anyone until I was sure that I was really seeing. One day as I sat on my bed, I turned my hands over in my lap several times, surprised that I could see them.

The next day I talked with Doctor Galt, who was also very excited about my progress. As soon as the doctor walked into my room, I knew it was him from the medicine smell. He was a large man with a big, warm smile that stretched across his face. He shone a light in each eye and gave me a veil to wear to shade my eyes when I went outdoors. He also said that my vision would continue to improve.

I even began hearing a little with my one good ear. But I still felt sad and lonely for my family. I never saw my father again. An empty spot was left inside of me because I did not tell him good-bye or kiss him back when he kissed me.

Earaches and infections continued to come and go. Sometimes a warm, brownish-yellow fluid would drip from my ear or I would find crust in my hair in the morning. I also became dizzy and sometimes my face became hot with fever.

Doctor Galt would treat me from time to time. In his small medical room he had a collection of supplies and medical equipment. A wooden box held glass bottles with cork stoppers. He also had small round glass balls with one open end that were used for collecting blood, and little shiny cutting gadgets that would open the skin to let bad blood come out. He used that one on me several times when I had terrible ear pain from the infection. These treatments upset me and made me feel weak, but in time my infections cleared up.

I learned that the hospital, which was now my home, was called the Eastern Lunatic Asylum. I cried when no one visited me because I knew that I might never see my family again. There were times that I did not care if I got better. The nights were the worst because I could sometimes hear screaming, crying, or begging. I could not make out all the words, but what I could hear sounded like grown people screaming out for their mothers, for food, or for help. That was the only time that I was glad that I could not hear very well. After a while, I woke up sometimes to find myself doing the same thing. When I cried, no one ever came to me, and months turned into years.

I was thankful that my eyes healed well, but my hearing was very poor on my best days, and I was often gloomy. Although Doctor Galt had nearly 300 patients, he noticed me because I was so much younger than most of the others. He told the staff to encourage me to begin accepting my condition. I liked the woman who cleaned our rooms, because she reminded me of Ellen. It made me feel useful when I helped with some of the daily duties, like sweeping and scrubbing. The doctor decided to let me go downtown during the day with some of the other women from the hospital.

Williamsburg's main busy street was just a short walk away,

down our road and around the corner, but it felt like a world apart from the asylum. Still, I did not have much interest in leaving the asylum at first—until I made friends with Rebecca. She was a new young patient, who could not talk. Rebecca had pale skin, blue eyes, and long blond curls. She was smaller than me. She must have been a few years younger than I was. Her not talking was fine with me, because I could hardly hear anyway. She would stay at my side, making us both feel better.

I thought to myself that Rebecca and Doctor Galt were as close as I could find to a real family. She was like a little sister who needed me and he was like a kind uncle. Doctor Galt let Rebecca go to town with me, and a few times we were given rides in his carriage. We would bounce down the road behind a dark chestnut horse, watching people, trees, and buildings as we passed. As we grew closer, Rebecca would hold my hand and smile at me.

We enjoyed going for walks to look at flowers. My favorite flowers were the violets, daisies, and black-eyed Susan that grew wild. If Rebecca noticed a new patch of flowers before I did, she would pull on my arm and point. I also loved the irises and gladiolas that grew in the ladies' flower gardens next to their homes.

My favorite tree in town was a red buckeye tree, because the hummingbirds would come to visit her red blooms in the spring. In the fall, nuts would cover the ground, as they fell from branches. Rebecca and I loved the fruit-bearing trees, because they smelled sweet in spring and we could later find something good to eat. We stopped to visit other flowering trees and evergreens along our way.

We loved to watch the birds, bunnies, squirrels, and other creatures as they played and searched for food. We visited with some of the pets and working animals that lived in town.

Some days, Rebecca and I watched the shoemaker who would smile at us or the silversmith who was so busy making shiny goblets, platters, and silverware that he hardly ever noticed us. We would go to Market Square to watch vendors selling their goods. In nice weather they would display some of their goods outdoors.

Occasionally prisoners were taken to a building down the street from the carpenter's shop. I was afraid to go near there because once I saw several men take an Indian inside the building. His clothes were torn and he was bleeding from his back, face, and arms. I wondered what else they were going to do to him and whether he had done something deserving of such a punishment. It was during those times that I hoped that my father was still alive and would come back for me soon.

Rebecca and I would walk down to see the Governor's Palace. I made believe that it was my home, along with its garden and horses. I could smell the turkey and cakes cooking inside and saw pumpkin pies sitting on the wide kitchen window ledge to cool. The wheelwrights would be pounding on wood and metal as they kept their fire burning hot. I could imagine my husband sitting with me by the fireplace, as I sewed and our children played in the yard.

Rebecca and I liked to watch many different people around town. We saw students from the school, at times, sitting in the shade of trees reading their books, talking with friends, or eating their lunch. The name of the school was the same as my parents, William and Mary, and it was located a few blocks from the asylum.

A few of the town ladies were nice to us and would occasionally give us little treats. One lady let us sit in her yard to watch her play with her baby. It was exciting to watch as the little one learned to walk and play with her mama. She reminded me of little Sarah Ann, Scotty, and Simeon. I had helped them when they learned to walk, talk, feed, and dress themselves.

I realized that I loved children and hoped to have children

of my own. I hoped that I would have a daughter first and that I would live a long life so I could stay with her as long as she needed me. Watching this young child gave me peace and hope for my future. I wondered whether I was just wishing and dreaming or whether I could truly have a chance at life outside the hospital.

As we walked further, Rebecca and I also saw Negro men, women, and children working in tobacco fields. They wore straw hats to block the sun's heat baking their dark skin. Some workers wore cloth tied around their heads to catch their sweat.

I could not understand how some groups of people could own other groups of people just because of their color. Why could not everyone live and work together in peace, just as our people had done? Older people should have time to rest, and new mothers should have time to care for their precious little ones.

Spring, summer, and harvest were busy times, with people working in their yards and on their houses or going to the open market. Town was much less active in winter when people were trying to keep warm. Rebecca and I searched for tracks or made our own in the snow.

Some evenings after our day in town, Rebecca and I would walk back to the hospital, stopping every couple of steps. We could see the cupola and weather vane on top of the hospital building from a distance. It was easier to see in the winter, with fewer leaves on the trees. As we walked up the path to the two-story red brick building with big doors, we saw a fence around the courtyard. We then stepped into what felt like a darker world than the one outside.

The matron would welcome us back to our room, locking the big secure doors behind each of us. My room had a bed, small desk with a wooden chair, two pegs for my clothes, and a chamber pot for me to use during the night. I could look out into the courtyard from my barred window and see a little bit of the long corridor from a barred section at the top of my door if I carefully balanced on the top of the back of my chair. In one way I liked the door to be locked to make me feel safe, but at the same time I did not like being unable to leave, even though I had no place to go anyway.

There was an iron chain and ring that hung from the wall near my bed that must have been used in the past as a restraint for an uncontrollable patient. I moved my bed a little to hide it. There were two dungeon-like cells dug under the building for patients who arrived in a state of uncontrollable anger.

What scared me most were the electrostatic machine that could be used to shock us and the tranquilizer chair that prevented us from moving. I had never been shocked or restrained in the chair and I made sure to be quiet and calm so I would not have to experience them.

Some patients did not know how to calm themselves, so they received these harsh treatments. I never saw the electrostatic machine in use but I did see patients sitting and staring at nothing after returning from their treatment.

I did see the tranquilizer chair being used, though. Angry, dangerous patients were held down by hospital workers and placed in the chair. Patients would scream, kick, swing, and bite to avoid sitting in that chair, but sooner or later they were strapped down one limb at a time. Then the big strap went around their arms and chest and a box would be lowered over their head. They had to face forward to see out of a small opening. Their gown would be pulled up in back so they could relieve themselves in the potty below. The harder they resisted, the more exhausted they became and often fell asleep after a time in the chair.

Doctor Galt tried other treatments as well. But I was lucky. I never had to take harsh drugs like the others or have blistering salve on my skin. There were also cold plunge baths, especially for the wild patients. I also remember that Rebecca cried after Doctor Galt had placed her in the ducking chair, lowering her into a deep tub of ice-cold water. She returned to me all wet and shivering. As I wrapped my blanket around her to make her warm, I thought that Doctor Galt tried this treatment to encourage Rebecca to start talking, but it did not work.

Granddaughter, even though he used these harsh treatments, I believe that the doctor tried to help and encourage his patients. He did the best he could. He was not a mean person, and several times, I saw him smiling and talking with visitors as he showed them around the hospital.

Doctor Galt started a library, game room, and the carpentry and shoemaking shops. Rebecca found a book in the library that had lots of pictures of birds, bugs, trees, and plants. She and I often took it with us to the woods, matching the creatures and plants to the pictures in the book.

I would ask the doctor to tell us the names of some of the plants. He drew circles for us around the pictures of the plants so we learned which ones we could eat, and we would go out to find them. We brought some back for the cook, who showed us how to prepare them. We made sure to leave some plants behind so new plants would grow the next year. I had learned that practice from my father.

Occasionally there were evening lectures at the asylum, which I avoided. But Rebecca and I attended the concerts and social events. Townspeople would perform on special occasions. The ladies looked so fine in their lovely full dresses with ruffles and puffy sleeves. Their hair was done up so pretty under bonnets. The men were handsomely dressed in suits as they walked with their heads held tall. Rebecca smiled when she saw some men who held one hand over their belly. We did not know why they did that but we thought it was funny. When no one was looking, she would put her hand on her stomach and lift her chin up towards me with her eyes blinking just to make me laugh.

I learned that I could hear the music by feeling the vibration of the instruments. If I sat close enough to the musicians or if I slipped my shoes off, I could feel the beat in the wooden floors. Rebecca and I learned the slow, quick, quick—slow, quick, quick beat of the waltz, and she and I would dance off to the side of the room.

We put on long shawls so they could float and glide through the air as we twirled and weaved around each other. At the end of the concerts, the people from town went back to the comfort of their homes and we would return to our dreary rooms, remembering the good time and nice people.

Rebecca liked going to the special sewing room. There we sewed, spun, and wove. I felt good that Willie had taught me how to darn and I was able to show my friend and some of the other women. These activities were very nice, but the screaming and moaning all around us reminded me that the Eastern Lunatic Asylum was still a home for insane patients.

There were too many patients and not enough workers to keep the place clean. Occasionally patients would attack one another. They would screech, scratch, slap, and bite. One lady would spit on me if I came too close. Another lady liked to sit or lie on the floor, tripping anyone who walked by too closely. I quickly learned to stand my ground because I did not want to be harmed. But I also did not want to be seen as being unfriendly because I was afraid my actions would cause others to hurt me.

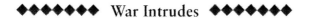

◆◆◆◆◆◆◆ War Intrudes ◆◆◆◆◆◆◆

A bigger problem was on its way for Williamsburg, the hospital, and its patients. The problem was the Civil War. On

May 6, 1862 Union troops moved into the area. Battles raged as the Southern troops retreated towards Richmond. Many of the townsmen were gone, except for the older gentlemen and young boys.

We became very agitated when we heard the constant firing of the guns and the bugles blowing just down the street. The noise was so loud that I could hear the shots as well. All patients were left in their rooms that fateful morning, with their doors locked and no breakfast served.

I was looking out my window as several of the workers were fleeing the property. Before they left the building I thought I heard one of them yell that Doctor Galt was dead. I hoped that I had heard wrong this time. We sat in our rooms all day with nothing to eat. We could not even empty our chamber pots.

Night was even worse. We were frightened and hungry and thirsty and dirty. The screams and pounding would not stop. Some patients must have been beating their doors with furniture. I felt the vibrations throughout the building. Days passed and I could not stand the odors, which left a stinging burn in my nose and made my stomach feel uneasy, causing my head to ache. After a while, it became very quiet, too quiet.

Union soldiers came into the hospital from time to time and walked around the grounds. I saw them peeking between the bars on my door. I hurried to hide against the wall. Soldiers shook and pounded on my door but they could not open it.

Mr. Sommersett Moore, one of the hospital workers who left, returned to the asylum a few weeks later. I guess that he wanted to help us because we were starving. He gave the keys to the Union soldiers. And this time when the soldiers returned, they opened my door. I ran down the hall to Rebecca's room, only to see that her door was open, but she was gone. I did not know what happened to her. I loved and needed her. All that was left again were memories like too many times before.

Suddenly two soldiers grabbed me from behind and dragged me back to my room. They shoved me onto my bed and told me not to move, or they would lock me in there till I died. I lay on my bed, staring out the window at the gray sky, wishing that I could just fly away like an eagle. I would go far up into the sky and glide, leaving every trouble far beneath me. I could not let myself think about what was happening to me.

The days of my life were flashing through my mind. I saw myself walking with my mother through the creek water, Father carrying me away from home, Aunt Lizzy working on the farm, Willie and Elya sleeping next to me in the loft, Uncle lying in the garden, Aunt Lizzy leaving, the children being born, Ellen talking with me, and Father whipping me.

These two soldiers smelled of sweat, and their stale breath tasted like salt and burnt tobacco. I could feel buttons digging into my flesh, as they rubbed back and forth. I was not sure why they wanted to do the things they were doing or why this was happening to me. I could not open my eyes again until long after they were gone. The pain of the day made me forget my growling hunger until late that evening when one of the ladies from town showed up and helped clean and feed me.

After a while Mr. Moore had the keys again. And I saw some patients leaving the hospital. A few must have died in their rooms because I saw them through my window as they were being carried out for burial. Mr. Moore came to my room late one evening to talk with me. He asked whether I thought I could find my way home to my family. He did not have enough help to take care of all the patients, and soldiers had raided the supplies. Realizing that this chance was what I had long been waiting for, I told him that I could do it.

Mr. Moore told me that he could not keep me any longer

if I wanted to leave. He said that I would have to stay out of sight and be very careful. He gave me a couple of rolls, some hardtack, and a haversack for my journey. I also took my library book, a piece of rope from the clothesline, some thread and needles from the sewing room, the blanket from my bed, and a sharp knife that I had taken from the kitchen the day after the soldiers left. I put my nightshirt on, with my day dress and my good dress on top so my bundle would be small.

He told me that Union soldiers were standing guard at the campus of the College of William and Mary. They had burned down one of the buildings. Other soldiers had taken valuables from some of the houses in town. He also told me that they had broken down fences for firewood. Soldiers were helping themselves to whatever they wanted. The military guards were watching the Williamsburg residents, and no one was allowed to come or go without permission.

Mr. Moore told me to say that I was lost if the soldiers saw me and that I was from the asylum. He figured that they might just bring me back. I told him that I knew every step of the entire area from all my outings and that I could get through without being seen. I had no doubt that going was better than staying; I needed to leave.

My Escape (1862-1863)

I was free. And I felt weightless as I walked through the big doors of the asylum at daybreak for my last time on that warm June morning. I had not slept all night, thinking, planning, wishing. I knew where I was going, so I kept walking past the front gate, never looking back. I walked with my small bundle in my arms and my head high until I was well out of sight.

I remembered everything that Aunt Lizzy had said before she left me many years earlier. She was so excited about going to Cincinnati because 'Everyone was welcome there.' She talked about the steamboats, trains, businesses, stores, jobs, and all kinds of people, including Indians, who were moving there to start a new life.

Granddaughter, I needed a new life, too. I was prepared. When I was young, I learned from my father how to travel safely, hide, and locate food. My library book from the hospital would also help me. I had to survive to keep my dreams alive. That is what Mother would have wanted.

I tried not to think too much about Father because it hurt me when I did. Something must have happened to him, or he would have come back to me at the hospital. I wondered whether he had decided to join the war. I could not go looking for the past. I had to look for the future.

My first night on my own challenged me but it made me more determined. As the sky turned dark, I was much more aware of my lack of hearing. I kept my eyes open wide to take in every movement around me. I sniffed the air to check for any new smells. Many large clouds covered the heavens above me, and a drizzly, cool rain soaked through all my belongings. But later towards morning I could see two distant morning stars sparkling through the darkness. Feeling them watching over me, I knew that I was not alone. A short time later, I saw a beautiful white dove flying west, showing me the way. I followed, staying near the railroad tracks that ran west and then northwest.

The land and creatures were beautiful. I loved to watch orange-and-black butterflies as they dined on milkweed plants, and the smaller yellow-and-black ones sipping on flowers. The forests were full of life from floor to canopy. I passed through woodlands, meadows, and wetlands, watching fireflies, raccoons, squirrels, and deer. I saw scarlet birds with black masks and red beaks; black bears, sometimes with one or two cubs; and olive colored fish in cool springs. Bugs of all kinds and colors crawled on plants and flew through the air. Tiny ants built homes in the reddish-brown dirt. Watching brave soaring eagles gave me courage and a feeling of harmony.

I avoided all the wide trails where someone might approach from behind, catching me unprepared. I passed huge plantations that looked like little towns. My steps were small and steady, and I walked along the tall grasses to stay hidden. While I walked, I looked down so I would not land on snakes or critters along my way. I remembered the sound of rattlesnakes I had heard as a child, but that was a sound that I could no longer hear, so my eyes had to protect me from disturbing them.

It was a good thing that I had a special way with animals, dogs in particular. This ability to communicate saved me a few times. Dogs would sprint, barking after me. When I turned around, I could see their mouths jerking open, showing their teeth. Their bodies jolted as though they were choking. I would talk to them and sing softly to calm them. They would stop their barking to hear what I was doing. Then I would send them back home.

In the evenings a peaceful feeling came over me as I watched deer searching for food and water. They would look at me with their shiny doe eyes before slipping out of sight. Some were more timid than others. I rarely saw the bucks.

When I needed help with directions, I would watch any strangers from a distance and choose the right person and the right time to ask. I tried to find older women because they were easiest for me to talk to and understand. I did not want to take a chance with any men who could hurt me like the two soldiers in the blue coats back in Williamsburg.

One early morning I came across two Indian women, who were watching me from a distance as I was watching them. After believing I was no threat, one of the women approached slowly, followed by the other one. We were aware of every movement around us. A bird flew past and the woman in front turned her head with a start in that direction and then back to me. I could see by the baskets they carried that they were on a search for food.

We tried to communicate with words but were not able to do so. So I pointed to myself and then the direction that I was headed. The older women pointed to herself and then in another direction. I nodded that I understood. They shared some berries with me and I shared some nuts before we parted. After walking a few steps away from them, I thought that I should join the women. But I decided that was not my destiny.

As I continued on my journey, plantations changed into farmhouses and cabins. Not wanting to be seen, I crawled on my hands and knees and found some food at the edges of farmers' fields, usually cucumbers, beans, and apples. Even though my stomach told me that I was hungry, sometimes I just could not eat because I felt sick.

I had traveled many miles through fields, past farms, down paths, over hills and mountains, and around cypress swamps. I even had to swim or wade across cold waters. It was good that Father had taught me so much about animal droppings, paw prints, and other signs in the forest, so I could make it on my own.

What he had not taught me, I learned from my sense of smell, which kept me away from trouble. I could tell when soldiers were near because I could smell cooked or discarded food, tobacco smoke, or sweat, which reminded me of the odors of the patients back where I had come from. That smell would stay in my nose and sometimes it would also make me feel sick in my stomach.

As the golden, red, and brown leaves fell from the trees, and the cold made my face and hands tingle, I knew that I had my own baby growing inside me. No one had ever talked with me about how to get a baby, but I had seen several births. I could see that my belly was getting bigger and my breasts were getting heavier. My moon time had stopped some time ago. I thought that this must have been how it was for Ellen, Willie, and Mother— all mothers—even animal mothers.

In many ways, Granddaughter, we are much like the wolf and bear. I saw Sarah Ann and Scott and Simeon born back on the farm. I even helped when Scott was born because Ellen was sick at that time and Willie needed me. There was much that I did not understand about life but I was ready to learn. I had seen puppies born and chicks hatch from eggs. Life all around me was so amazing. I wondered when my baby would be ready to come out to see me, but I also hoped that we would not be alone.

Cold and hungry, I always knew that I had to keep

moving, for both myself and my baby. Even though the blanket of snow soaked my feet right through my shoes, I was happy because I had always wanted a baby, and I thought about Ellen's children and about my mother and how she cared for me.

As I continued on my journey, a few women invited me in to eat and rest in their homes. One woman even gave me a coat and gloves. I would leave as soon as I thanked them for their kindness and asked for directions. My resting was done in out-of-the-way spots among trees. I remembered my father telling me that the trees were the chiefs of the plants. I felt much safer when they provided me with protection.

I told the trees that Cincinnati was my destination. I also talked to many different animals that I passed along the walk. A number of them chattered, squawked, or barked back to me. They would warn me with their actions if someone was approaching while I rested.

Often in the silence of the night I thought I could hear distant wolves howl but maybe it was in my memory of sounds. Anyway it somehow made me think of my mother's love and how much I missed her.

Only once on my trip did I actually look right into the eyes of a wolf. We were both searching for food along the edge of a rocky creek and were shocked to see each other. Her head and ears perked instantly, and she stood frozen for a moment as did I, but she blinked her blazing eyes, turned, and disappeared behind thick bushy pines, rocks, and shrubs. My body, tense, and my face, hot, I could feel my heart beating. She probably had babies to protect, as I was ready to protect mine. I sloshed across to the other side of the creek to continue my search for food.

From time to time, I would see smoke rising in the air. I knew it was coming from the guns and cannons because I could feel the vibration each time they exploded and see the jolting wings of birds and bodies of creatures. I steered clear of those areas, but sometimes I had to pass through fields and forests where I saw soldiers lying in puddles of their own dark blood.

The first bloody sight of bodies lying on the ground made me close my eyes, as I passed so I would not have to look at their faces. Early in my journey, I saw men sprawled out among the black-eyed Susan. I also saw men lying among the underbrush. Toward the end of my travels, I saw other soldiers covered with snow, lying among red-stained ferns or lifeless brown leaves and grasses. Often I saw vultures and flies circling above bodies.

But after seeing so many bodies, I learned to accept death as the last part of life and even found that I had become a little curious about the dead men. I wondered who would be sad about their not returning home to the family. Most of these men must have had a mother, wife, or someone who loved them. Sometimes I wondered whether my father could be among them and I looked for his face. I did not find him.

◆◆◆◆◆◆ More Soldiers ◆◆◆◆◆◆

At all times I had to be alert. After all, I had to survive. One time, I took a pair of shoes from a young dead soldier. Mine were worn out, and he no longer had need of his. I stuffed grass inside to make them warmer and fit better.

Another time I found a thin white horse wearing a saddle and wandering around. I rode him for two nights and fixed him to a branch away from my hiding place as I rested. Finally I decided to set him free because I felt safer walking. As it began to snow and I was about to undo the horse's straps from the branch, I saw a tattered Southern soldier limping up the road. I slipped behind a tree where I could watch safely. The young man was using a stick to aid his walking, and as he limped, loose bloody bandages tied around his leg flapped in a slow rhythm.

When I saw that he was alone, I decided that he could not harm me. Approaching, I held onto the horse's rein, prepared to run—even in my condition—at the first sight of trouble. I stared into his face and eyes for any sign that he wanted to harm me. Sure that I was safe, I walked the horse up to him, and I helped him mount.

Not a word was spoken between us, but I saw a slight smile of relief grow on one side of his face as he took a deep breath. He lifted his fingers to his hat brim and tilted his head toward me. He pulled a golden broach from his pocket and looked at it for a while. Maybe it had belonged to his mother or wife. Dropping it to the ground before me, he slowly rode away. After grabbing it, I slipped quickly back into the snowy grasses for cover.

One sunrise while walking along the edge of the road, I saw something shining in the mud. I looked in both directions before darting out to see what it was. I found a golden watch and chain, which I lifted from the cold mud and wiped it off. I hung the chain from the side of my belt, which I had braided from strips of material I had found in the hospital sewing room.

I came up to a young girl who was sitting by a river; she had a boat. As I pointed to the other side, she said something that I did not understand. I showed her the watch. She nodded as she took it and I climbed into the boat and we crossed the river. I was so glad that I did not have to swim through that cold current, around the floating ice, and soak all my things again.

Early one morning, I found a man with legs stretched out on the ground and his back leaning against a tree. His eyes were shut and his mouth, open but twisted. From my hiding place behind a tree, I saw he was holding a gun in his lap. His face reminded me of Uncle Will. I did not see any blood, so I watched the stranger for a while, making sure that he was not just sleeping.

Then I threw a few stones nearer and nearer to him until one landed right on his chest. He did not move, so I inched more closely. A bundle was lying next to him. When I opened it, I saw a warm coat, a blanket, and a full package of salty hardtack.

I gave thanks by nodding my head to the man who had left me these gifts and looked up toward Heaven to thank my Creator as I started to eat. My mouth was watering as I reached in for another piece but the food did not want to go down. I thought I had felt my baby move, and I had to stop eating until that strange feeling passed. I worried that she was going to die. But I had to keep moving because the winter winds started to howl and the sky began to darken.

Here I was, a grown woman, an Indian with no schooling. I could not read or write and I had spent several years in an asylum. I was still living in my same country, but it had somehow become the White Man's world. It seemed that he was busy fighting, killing, and making a mess of things. I had to think not about the bad but concentrate on the good things that I could do. I could take care of myself. I was good at caring for children. I could work in the garden, clean house, and cook all kinds of food. Also, I was pretty good at darning and sewing. I had even made clothes for some of the patients in the asylum.

I decided not to tell anyone about the asylum and all the things that happened there, because other people might not understand. How could anyone understand when I did not understand much about it myself?

Often I had dreams as I traveled. I dreamt of the stars, moon, and seasons changing over and over, making me think that I would have a long, long walk on Mother Earth. Sometimes I saw myself as a warrior princess making my way through many trials of life. I loved my dreams because in them I could clearly hear the wind blowing, waterfalls rushing, birds singing, and my mother's voice. She sang in her soft, low, comforting tone—the sweetest sound of all I had ever known.

It is funny, Granddaughter, how many of these beautiful sounds can be taken for granted. My life outside the hospital was much different now and I was never going back. I made sure to get me and my baby far away. I would never take my baby there. No, not ever! I put my hands on my stomach, as I made that promise to her.

I could get a job and money like Father did so I could take good care of my baby in Cincinnati. I believed that I would have a daughter and I already knew what to name her. Her name would be Margaret Ann and I would call her Maggie. That was the name of the precious little baby in Williamsburg. She and her mother were happy together, as we would be. One of the biggest things that I was looking forward to was hearing my baby call me, *Mama*. I hoped to keep enough hearing for that.

Granddaughter, it is almost morning and you will soon be starting your busy day. I have enjoyed our time together, but I must leave you now. I will return in your dreams another night to tell you more of my story.

Maternal Lineage:
Mary Ann Cox

3rd Great - grandmother	First Husband	Year Married	Children
Mary Ann Penn (1838-1924)	Abner Cox (1838-1870)	1865	Maggie (1863-1913) Daniel (1867-1949) Elizabeth (1870-1870)

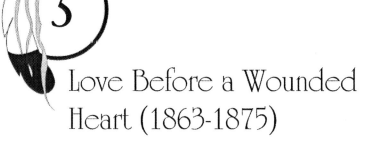

5

Love Before a Wounded Heart (1863-1875)

Granddaughter, I have come again to speak to you. There is still much that I have to share and will tell you all that I can. During my last visit I told you about my young life, my escape from the asylum, and the long journey to Cincinnati. That was just the beginning.

It was late winter when my journey finally ended and the snow had begun melting. I crossed over the Ohio River on a ferryboat, which moved very slowly so it would not hit any of the chunks of ice in the river. I paid for my trip with the gold broach that the soldier had given me. The man on the ferry held out his hand for more, but I just looked at him because that was all I had. After looking at me funny, he nodded his head back over his shoulder to motion me aboard. People were pushing behind me in line so I moved on. Many women were holding the hands of their young children. I did not know that so many people existed.

As the ferry was getting closer to the waterfront, I saw steamboats spraying huge white billows into the sky as they moved up the river to unload passengers. These boats looked like they were making puffy white clouds for the blue sky. The big round wheels turning on the back of some boats made the water splash and foam.

Everywhere I looked there were people. I saw White Men

and Orientals and Negroes as well as Indians. Most of them were carrying their life's possessions on their backs or under their arms in bundles. Many, just like me, arrived by boat and walked down wooden planks on to the shore. Most of these people wore dirty, ripped clothes. Some were with their families; some were alone. But they had made it to Cincinnati.

Ohio had remained a free state throughout the Civil War. Because there was no fighting in Ohio as there was in Virginia, Cincinnati was a safe place. And Aunt Lizzy was always talking about how it was a good place for Indians. She also said that there were people living there called Friends, who did not believe in slaves or war. The Friends just wanted to help runaway slaves make a new life.

Resting for a moment on a bench, I placed my things in my lap. I started thinking how proud my mother and father would have been of my long trip, when I was startled by the loud sound of a train whistle and a screeching noise that announced the arrival of a train in a station near the waterfront. When the whistle blew, even my baby poked me. By now I knew that the baby was just moving inside me and I was not afraid.

I had seen many trains in Virginia. Father called them locomotives. I saw some carrying tobacco, corn, apples, pigs, and lumber. Even on my journey I saw a couple of trains loaded with soldiers. One time I saw soldiers in blue uniforms pounding and pulling to destroy train tracks.

This was not a time for daydreams. I was tired and needed something to eat. I would have to find a safe place to sleep before night set in. There were signs everywhere, and how I wished I could read them because I did not know which way to go. Many people were chattering around me, but it was hard to make out what they were saying.

I now saw what Aunt Lizzy had meant about people helping the escaped slaves. I saw people who reached out their hands to Negroes as they passed. The nice people just walked away with the newcomers. About that time a lady looking in my direction walked towards me. She stood right before me, talking, but I could not make out any of the words. Her face showed so much tenderness that I rose from the bench and went with her.

I could not believe what happened next. She took me to a huge, warm house with many rooms. I thought I smelled fish and bread baking. My mouth began watering when I saw so much food on a table. My baby started to move again, and I reached out for the lady's hand to lay it against my body. A big smile came on her face and I realized that I could read her lips as she said, 'Yes, I know. You are going to have a baby! Your tummy is out to here,' she said, rounding her arms in front of her stomach. 'Just sit here and eat while I get you some water. You will be safe here. We will help you.'

I took a bite of bread and nearly choked on it. She smiled, left the room, and returned with a beautiful pair of shoes, which she set on the bench next to me. My shoes were nothing more than bits and pieces. I had cuts and scars on my swollen feet. I felt so happy and relieved that a tear rolled down my cheek, as I nodded my thanks to her.

I later learned that the nice lady, Mrs. Carol, also a Friend, ran the house. Many other people stayed there, too. But they never stayed longer than a day or two. Mrs. Carol let me stay longer because it was almost time for my baby. I helped with cooking and cleaning. And she taught me how she liked things done. I also helped new people by sewing patches on their clothes to cover up holes. I tried to make others feel welcomed as I had felt when I first came to live there.

◆◆◆◆◆◆◆ Maggie's Birth ◆◆◆◆◆◆◆

Late one evening after dinner, as I was washing dishes, I had a cramp that would not go away. I stopped my work several times just to rub my back and walk around. By the time I was finished in the kitchen, I noticed a puddle of water where I stood. My labor had started, and the pains lasted all night and into the next morning. On March 15, 1863, my daughter Maggie was born. She was the most precious baby I had ever seen. I was the proudest woman in Cincinnati. And then I thought that I was the proudest mother on Earth.

I rested while Mrs. Carol and some of the other women changed my bedding after the birth and helped me change clothes. They also washed and dressed the baby and later brought me something to eat. One of the women who had nursed her baby gave me a few tips to help me know what to do.

I waited for late evening, when everyone else had gone to bed, and I carried Maggie outside. Then I opened her blanket to reveal her tiny oval face and lifted her up to the starry sky. I spoke to Mother in my spirit voice and hoped that she could see me with her first-born granddaughter. I then realized that I could faintly hear Maggie cry as I held her little mouth softly against my right ear. I could hear certain sounds if they were close or very loud. I had no hearing at all in my other ear.

This was only the second time that I felt so much joy. The first time was when I left Virginia to start my long journey and my new life. Now I was living it. My hands were almost numb and my heart was pounding with love. I was no longer alone.

◆◆◆◆◆◆◆ Abner Cox ◆◆◆◆◆◆◆

When Maggie was two years old, I met a young man named

Abner Cox. The Civil War had just ended, with the North conquering the South. Things were getting back to normal. Abner was a hardworking, handsome dark-skinned Delaware Indian.

His grandmother's people had moved from Pennsylvania, the home of the English Quaker, William Penn, to a Delaware Indian Reservation in Xenia, at the mouth of the Little Miami River and Beaver Creek in central Ohio. His grandmother married a Shawnee man and after a few years they moved to Greenville, Ohio, where Abner's mother was born.

His mother traveled down the river to Cincinnati to sell goods with her father. That is where she met and married Abner's father, a man from Virginia. Abner was an only child, growing up along the Ohio River. Working with his father, they did all kinds of jobs, but they mostly put roofs on new houses.

Abner came by Mrs. Carol's house to do some carpentry repairs. Dressed in overalls, he had some tools and nails hanging in a pouch he wore around his waist. A dark-blue cap blocked the sun while he worked on the roof. Granddaughter, he loved that cap, which was a gift from his father.

It was a civilian slouch hat, the same kind as the Civil War soldiers wore, except the civilian cap did not have any emblem. And it also came in many colors. Abner's dark-blue one faded over the years, with the top of the broad brim turning to more of a gray, although the underside was still blue. Abner and I talked about the two colors because they were the ones worn by the Southern and Northern troops—all on the same hat.

There were two rows of stitching and he had added a hat-band ribbon around the base of the cap. I repaired the hat a few times, stitching here and there to keep the brim from coming loose. He loved that cap and wore it like a crown until the day he passed over.

At lunchtime he came inside to eat. He loved my cooking,

smiled a lot, and played with Maggie. I could not help but see his muscles as he lifted her. At the end of the day when he was finished with his work, he stopped in to say good-bye. I watched out the window as he walked away. I could feel a stirring like butterflies inside my body and wondered whether I would see him again. I started thinking that he might be a good father for my Maggie.

The next morning, as I was up early making breakfast, I saw Abner walking to the front door. He said that he was missing a hammer that he needed for his next job. I helped him look around the house and we finally found the hammer lying on the floor close to the front-porch door. I wondered whether he had left that tool there the day before or just that morning.

He smiled again and asked whether he could come back to see me that evening after work. I told him that I was totally deaf and had not heard a single sound for quite a while, although I had already read his lips and knew exactly what he had said. I just wanted to see his words again. When he repeated his question, I smiled and nodded my head, trying not to show the excitement that I felt buzzing through my body. I walked him out to the front yard.

I could smell the dew of the morning, as I took a deep breath and watched him walk away. When he reached the end of the block, he looked back and raised his hand to wave to me before turning the corner. The bright blue sky and dew smelled so fresh—like a new start. I felt the same way as I had the morning that I left the hospital for good.

Abner started to come by each evening, and we would sit for hours on the front steps to watch the evening sky. Sometimes we would talk. Abner always told me how pretty I looked. He especially liked the way I wore my hair in one braid down my back.

He knew that I had a baby and that I was living there

without a husband. He told me later that he thought my husband had passed away. But I explained to him what had happened to me during the war. He told me that Maggie was a beautiful child brought into the world as a result of the war.

One night when Abner did not come by at his usual time, I worried that something had happened to him. Long after Maggie had fallen asleep, I sat on the steps, waiting. Finally, I saw him coming down the road. Smiling, he walked up to me, looked into my eyes, reached for my hand, and placed a small gold band in the center of my palm and closed my fingers around it. He then asked me to be his wife. Granddaughter, his eyes showed me that he was sure that I would say yes. He was right.

We were married the next week. Maggie and I said good-bye to the nice people who had helped us. Mrs. Carol was sad to see us go, but at the same time she was very happy for our new life.

Abner already had a small home that he had built in the 3rd Ward of Cincinnati, one of the wards close to downtown. He told me that he had plans to build another room. In fact, he had already collected supplies for the project.

He was a good husband and a patient father to Maggie, who loved being with him. She would watch for him to come home from work so he could play with her. She liked to sit on his lap and talk with him. She always kissed him good night before she went to bed. In 1867, when Maggie was four years old, Abner and I had a baby boy, and we named him Daniel.

Daniel looked nothing like Maggie. She was pale skinned with brown hair and light-green eyes, just like your eyes, Grand-daughter. Daniel had black hair, dark eyes, and very dark skin like his father's. Another baby, Elizabeth, was born in 1870. She also looked much like Abner. Elizabeth was named after my Aunt Lizzy. I had hoped to find her in Cincinnati, but I just knew her

61

as Aunt Lizzy. The only person who had her address was my father, and I did not know where he was. Everywhere I went, I looked for Aunt Lizzy, but there were so many people. I had no luck.

We had a happy home and Abner worked hard to supply our needs. We enjoyed being together and I was happy to live in our own place. He was everything I could hope for in a husband. It was such a great feeling to be loved like that.

Before Elizabeth's first birthday, Abner came home sick from work. He was running a fever and went right to bed. I fed him soup, washed him, and tried to keep him warm as he shivered. Several of our neighbors were also sick. I left him only once to nurse the baby and put her in bed with Maggie.

When I fell asleep, it was almost morning. I dreamt of my mother, who was standing on the side of Blue Mountain, singing a prayer, with a strong breeze blowing her long, dark hair. She stopped singing to call my name. It woke me suddenly and I reached over to check on Abner, only to find him lying still at my side. I could not believe that my Abner had passed on as I slept. I thought that we would grow old together.

When I checked on the children that morning, I saw that Elizabeth also had the fever. She had not even cried. Her body was hot and her eyes looked dull. She would not nurse. When I tried to give her drips of water with a spoon, she choked and spit up, trying to push the spoon away with her tiny hands. Two days later she also passed on.

It was too much to bear, but I still had Maggie and Daniel to care for. I learned that a mother cannot think of herself first, even when she is exhausted and in pain. She has to think of her children. I had to think of a good plan. Life was totally up to me again. I could not let my children down.

My pain was something that had to be put aside. I had to pull my shoulders back, lift my head up, and swallow hard. My swollen breasts were full, tight, and painful. My baby had taken my milk every three or four hours. And my body was set to the rhythm of feeding her. I wrapped ripped cotton strips around my breasts to stop the flow of my milk. But it continued to flow when it was time to feed, soaking my clothes. Each time I felt the milk, it reminded me of my loss. The cotton material left red marks under my arms and around my back, but finally my milk stopped flowing.

I learned how to appreciate even the smallest things in the midst of sorrow: scents of flowers, small creatures, the feel of someone's hand in mine, soaring birds, and a cup of tea. And, most of all, I appreciated my memories.

◆◆◆◆◆◆◆ **A Moment Remembered** ◆◆◆◆◆◆◆

Granddaughter, I often thought of my true love and how I missed him so. I treasured our moments together. Sometimes I would walk down to the water where I once sat with Abner, and my mind would wander to those beautiful moments:

As the sun pauses for a moment over the gold and blue water before its descent from this day, I find that I am humming— not to a song but to a moment past, a time and place remembered. I am looking into snowflakes dancing in the air—a place no one else has ever been, a place of peace and harmony—and my senses come alive.

I am younger and I try to take it all in. In the stillness I can hear a heartbeat—a heart of love—patient and forgiving. Was he really here? Did I let him go? Could I have done more? The sun has gone now and all is quiet, except for the lapping of water against the shore. The night slips in and brightly colored rays reach across the sky as to say good-bye. Only a part of you remains with me. Is it possible to ever find my way back to you?

After I buried my husband and baby, I had to pull myself together. I spent most of the family savings hidden in a jug under a floorboard to pay for the burials, food, and needed supplies. But I still had just enough left to buy a Singer sewing machine, which I had seen in the local general store.

The general store had a creaky floor with a black potbelly stove sitting in the center of the room. Many items were hanging from the walls and ceiling. Items such as ropes, knives, utensils, high button shoes, candles, suspenders, cow tonics, and tins of cloves were lined up on shelves.

Granddaughter, let me tell you what cow tonic is because you might not know. Cow tonics were sold in jugs to cure a variety of health problems including anemia, nose bleeds, gout, sleeping problems, muscle and bone aches, and acid stomach. Other tonics came with many promises such as long life and good health.

I had never seen so many supplies at one time in one store. The open wooden shelves held bean pots, long-handled water dippers, pails, lanterns, laxatives, tobacco, pipes, sewing kits, and salves that I could have used to soften my callused hands, but I did not have the money.

Tinware, spices, and silk ribbons were favorites of most ladies, but I will admit that my children and I loved the candy, like the peppermint sticks, maple-sugar candy, licorice, taffy, horehound, which is bitter mint, and rock candy. Different smells mixed, and the aroma of the fatty soap, leather, and food hung in the dusty air.

Mr. Jones, the owner, and his wife worked six days a week in the store. I could communicate with Mrs. Jones, but it was hard for me to understand her husband because of his beard; I could not see his lips very well.

Maggie helped me *hear*. She had learned to move her lips as others were talking so I could make out what they were saying. I did not like to look directly at people I did not know well or people who were not friendly. Maggie seemed to know when I needed help. She would stand between me and the person talking to me. Facing my daughter, I could see her lips as she told me what the person wanted. Maggie used fewer words, making it easier for me to understand what was being said.

Maggie needed a new dress, so I bought the sewing machine and sewing needles. I also bought a half bolt of cloth and a spool of thread on credit. I stayed up late that night, sewing her dress. When it was finished, I helped her put it on and took her with me to the store to show the owner's wife how pretty my Maggie looked. I also hoped that the owner could see my work and hire me to make dresses.

Mrs. Jones admired my sewing and agreed to supply me with material. She would give me a portion of the money that she would make from dresses sold. I did the same thing at two other stores where the owners agreed to hang dresses in their windows to sell. Giving stores my dresses to sell would be a way that I could make money to feed my children. A few of my close neighbors even bought dresses directly from me for themselves and their daughters.

I spent hours at my machine, making dresses. And it did not take long for the dresses to sell, which I replaced with new dresses. But the profit was just barely enough to cover all our living expenses. We were just getting by.

Mrs. Jones was very nice to us and even helped Maggie get started in school. Mrs. Jones told me that it was okay for Maggie to go to school because she looked White. But it was better not to take Daniel because his skin was so dark.

Even though Cincinnati was a place that welcomed many races, there were still some people who hated Indians, Orientals, and Negroes. Mrs. Jones said that some people would not accept

Daniel, and other children would probably be cruel to him. Sadly, I already knew that children teased him, so I just nodded my head to her. But I tell you, Granddaughter, that there are good and bad in all races.

I was thankful for people like Mrs. Jones. I had seen how some other people looked at us as we walked past. Even Mr. Jones looked at me strange sometimes. On many occasions, Maggie told me that people laughed or said bad words to us. I was sorry that my little girl had to experience this treatment, but I was so happy that she was learning to read and write. She would have better opportunities and more choices in life than I had.

Maggie loved school and was happy when Mrs. Jones would sometimes quiz her when we went to the store. Maggie wrote her name and other words in a tablet that Mrs. Jones had given her, filling every page with writing. That beautiful child even wrote with her finger in the dust or on steamy windows. She taught me and Daniel to write our names, too. Maggie insisted.

The White Man knew how to read and I wanted this skill for my girl. Maggie was proud as she started to read signs, labels, and notices. There had been so many things that I had not known or understood. Yet my young daughter knew so much just by glancing at words. It was wonderful and almost magical when she learned new things.

One day, I went into the general store to deliver a new dress and found out that dear Mrs. Jones had passed away. Maggie and I both felt very sad. Mr. Jones motioned to me to come into the back room. He wanted to show me some things that his wife left for me. When I went back there, I found that he was lying.

He shoved me against the wall, covered my mouth with one hand, and grabbed at my skirt. He whispered to be quiet by putting his pointer finger over his lips and giving me a harsh stare. His forehead wrinkled and his hands trembled. My heart nearly jumped out of my throat. I had seen men like this before. I was not quiet.

He thought that I would give what he demanded so I could continue selling my dresses in his store. He was mistaken. I screamed, grabbed a broom with my sweaty hands, raised my arms to act as if I would hurt him, but then I dropped the broom and ran out. I knew that if I had hurt him, there would have been much trouble for me. Who would have believed me over a man, a White man—a store owner with money? I thought about Father and how he was falsely accused of stealing.

Just like Mr. Dudley Smith, Mr. Jones could accuse me of stealing and not get caught lying. I had trouble with expressing myself clearly to people outside my small group of close friends and my children. I knew what words to say, but it had been so long since I had heard words that my speech was no longer clear. What would happen to my beautiful children? They would be lost without me to care for them. I knew not to say anything and just run.

I grabbed Maggie's hand as I ran through the store and out the door, dragging Daniel with me. When we all were across the street, Maggie told me that Mr. Jones was still yelling, 'Do not come back!' I was not thinking of going back there again, not even to get my dresses. I had come to know that my body was my own and that no man would take it without my approval. I had to protect myself and my children by being alert and ready to act wisely. That evening I had to think about other things that I could do to take care of my family.

I found a job working as a servant, cleaning and cooking twice a week. Later I took a second job doing the same thing. Daniel went with me to my first job. The other one was in the afternoon, so Maggie watched Daniel after school. I found jobs near our home that I could walk to and Maggie could come for me if she needed me.

Maggie, Daniel, and I celebrated when she finished her three years of schooling. Daniel and I gave Maggie a book of poetry to show how happy we were. I knew how much Maggie loved rhyming words that had rhythm like music. Watching her read reminded me of my younger days when I first learned to waltz. I wanted to give her more, but she was thankful for the gift and our joy. We walked down to the water's edge, spread out a blanket, and lay down to watch Maggie read. Between each poem, she would pause to look into my eyes and smile.

Maternal Lineage:
Mary Ann Penn Cox Holmes

3rd Great - grandmother	Second Husband	Year Married	Children
Mary Ann Penn Cox (1838-1924)	Benjamin Holmes (1821-1921)	1875	Mary (1876-1886) Albert (1878-1882)

6

Holding the Family Together (1875-1880)

Granddaughter, have you ever noticed that when you are not even searching, something wonderful can happen? About five years after my husband Abner and Baby Elizabeth passed on, I met a railroad man named Benjamin Holmes, a Choctaw, born in Mississippi in 1823.

When Ben was a boy, the Treaty of Dancing Rabbit Creek was signed. Thousands of Choctaw were forced to leave Mississippi and move to Oklahoma, which means *Land of the Red People*. Without enough food, blankets, and other goods, the Choctaw had to walk many days. Even the elderly and sick were forced to walk. Many starved or died from disease on their trip.

Ben's mother passed away at that time just after delivering a baby daughter. His father gave the baby to his wife's sister because he could not care for her. Knowing that Ohio would be a better life, Ben's father took his son to Cincinnati instead of moving to Oklahoma. He did not trust the White Man, who was taking Indians away. Ben's father had heard many stories about Cincinnati and he wanted to see it for himself.

Ben's first wife was an Algonquin girl named Flower Moon. They were together for many years, but they had no children. She passed away a few years before I met Ben, and he was living alone.

Taller and heavier than Abner, Ben was also older. In fact, he was 16 years older than me. His black hair had gray streaks and his hairline had already started to move back, showing more of his forehead. He wore his hair in a ponytail that he tucked into his shirt when he went to work.

I had been working as a servant at Ben's home cleaning, washing his clothes, and making his dinner once a week. He told me that he looked forward to seeing me because I made everything so nice and he loved my cooking. His favorite dinner was my chicken soup, a biscuit, and sweet-pan cooked apple.

Before eating, he would close his eyes and sniff the air above his bowl, enjoying the aromas in the house. I would smile, feeling my cheeks warm as I remembered that Abner would close his eyes the same way. Then I would quickly turn away when Ben opened his eyes so he would not see my face. Ben also enjoyed talking to me in the kitchen, as I finished cooking. He smiled a lot, revealing a front chipped tooth from a fall he took as a boy.

I had to stop what I was doing to look at him as he talked. I found that I could understand him easily and loved looking at how his face would change as he told his stories. He talked with his eyes and hands as much as with his mouth, showing me the size and shapes of things with both of his big callused hands. He tilted his head and smiled when he spoke of his mother. He must have loved her a lot because I could see it in his face and eyes.

I realized later that he must have hired me as a way to get to know me or, even more so, for me to get to know him. I would walk past his home when I went to work at his neighbor's house. I did not know it at the time, but he had asked her about me. She said that I was a hard worker and a great cook. He stopped me one day and asked whether I could come by his house once a week to clean and cook for him, too.

He was so patient that it was easy for me to talk with him.

If he did not understand what I was saying, he would touch my arm gently and ask me to repeat. After a short time he learned to understand. He explained that there were a few sounds that I no longer used and some I had changed. He said that for the word *are*, I just made a breath sound like blowing out a flame and I did not circle my lips wide enough.

Ben always dreamed of working on the railroad, and his boyhood dream finally came true. He worked cleaning train boilers—hard, dirty, and dangerous work, but he was careful and did not mind what he had to do. He worked every day in sun, rain, ice, or snow. Some of his duties included cleaning the smoke box, emptying the ash pan, and digging out the pit. Ben was glad to have a steady job with fair pay.

He wore a blue-and-white striped railroad cap, long, dark overalls, a long-sleeve shirt, heavy gloves, and steel-capped boots. In bitterly cold weather he also wore a short, black wool button-down outercoat that had two big pockets at the hips and more inside, which he called his donkey jacket. He loved it because it kept him so warm on cold days. In fact, sometimes he would wear it just in case the weather would turn cold.

After enjoying several of my dinners, Ben asked me to marry him. I was afraid at first, partly because he was so much older than me. Granddaughter, I did not even know he was thinking about me in *that way*, but I decided that it would be good for me and the children. So I married Ben in 1875, when Maggie was 12 and Daniel was eight.

We first lived on Hunt Street, but Ben found a nice house for sale closer to the train station on Miami Avenue in Madeira. Our three-room home was a red brick, *shotgun* house, which meant that if someone shot a gun through the front door, the bullet would go right through the house and out the back door. We had a basement and a small front porch. Many years later Ben and

Daniel built a shed in the backyard to hold all the tools, seeds, and other supplies used for the garden. Every summer we had a vegetable and flower garden in the side yard, where our family spent many hours.

Camargo Road was just a short distance up the hill, and the Madeira Train Station was about the same short distance down the hill. I could see both from the front yard. We could see train passengers arriving and departing. I could feel the trains through the wooden floors in the house before the train pulled into the station, and I would let Ben know that it was time to go to work. I loved our home because it kept us warm in winter and dry and safe all year long.

Ben told me that I would not have to work selling dresses or cleaning other houses. I could stay home to take care of him, our house, and the young ones. I was very thankful for his thinking about me.

Before we married, I had been struggling because the clothing industry was becoming popular, now that clothes could be produced in a factory. New fashions and a new dress shops in town made it difficult for me to sell as much as I had in the past. Some people were still buying my dresses, but not as many as before and I had to lower my prices.

Even though Ben was so much older than me, we started adding to our family. When I had a baby girl in 1876, Ben asked me whether I wanted to name her Mary Jane, after my mother because he knew how much I still missed her. Two years later we had a baby boy and we named him Albert, after Ben's long-passed father.

Ben was a wonderful husband and devoted father. He helped me around the house and yard whenever he could. All he asked was that I make him good meals and keep the house clean, which I was glad to do. He had an old chair in the backyard next to mine. We would sit there together in the evenings He would sip his dark-brewed coffee and when he finished, he would sometimes take a nap. Granddaughter, he loved his steaming hot cup of coffee, and I could smell when he was near without even turning around to see him.

◆◆◆◆◆◆◆ **The Storyteller** ◆◆◆◆◆◆◆

Ben showed the children how to fish and taught them about plants and animals. He never raised his voice like my son-in-law did later. And the children all loved Ben and knew that they could tell him anything. But what he especially liked doing was to tell them stories about his Mississippi home. And the children loved to listen.

Ben told them the story about his father and the honeybees. His father would take a few smoldering sticks to smoke the bees before taking a portion of their honey. One time he climbed a tree where the bees had their home. He went too far out on the branch, it cracked, and he dropped his smoke sticks. He lost his grip and started sliding down the tree taking the hive and bees with him. The bees were so mad that they stung him until he jumped into the river. It took awhile before he was hungry for more honey.

One of his other stories was about his mother, who loved the beautiful magnolia trees along the big river. She went there often when they were in bloom. It was there under the magnolia that she first met Ben's father.

Another story was about the red fox and the mockingbird. The children felt sorry for the poor fox, who was always being attacked by the mockingbird. The mockingbird and his mate had to make sure that their five eggs were protected, when he was busy finding insects and berries. He did not want the fox living in the hole at the base of the tree because the nest was in a low forked branch, and the mockingbird was afraid that the fox would get to the eggs. Attacking the fox again and again, the mockingbird forced the fox to find a new home and move away.

But the children's favorite story was about a young Ben and the skunk. The children would laugh as he told them about bringing home a skunk that he had caught in a trap. His mother screamed and yelled at him to take it far away. When he returned home a couple of hours later, he told her that he was sorry that he had been sprayed by his little black-and-white friend.

His mother told his sisters to make Ben a soak bath in a big pot, barely large enough for him to fit into, out in the yard while he burned his clothes. Ben's sisters wanted to take away the odor, so they put everything that they could think of that had a strong smell into the pot. Later everyone said he smelled worse than when he had gotten into the bath. He had to sleep outside, down-wind for two nights.

For some reason the younger children thought it was the funniest thing that they ever heard. They begged Ben to tell the same stories over and over, and they never tired of hearing them. Maggie and I enjoyed watching them laugh.

The children and I would watch for Ben to come home from work. Walking up the hill, he carried his lantern in one hand and a black metal lunch pail in the other. Before coming into the house he would stomp his feet and take his cap off to beat the soot off his clothes. He would have black smudges on his face, clothes, and hands. And I would have a pan of hot water ready on the stove for him to clean up and clothes for him to wear. He would give me his empty lunch pail, telling me how much he loved his treats.

Our street was a busy spot in town. Ben would walk down to see whether the trains needed cleaning. There was a little park area with a bench and a drinking well across the street from the station. A bucket and dipper hung there for passengers to get a cold drink. Stores and other business were close by. The population in Madeira was growing with each year. So were our children.

I see that it is almost morning. The sun is starting to cast a little light into the eastern sky so I must leave you again. Go back to your bed, Granddaughter. I shall return another night to tell you more of my story.

7
A Beautiful Wedding (1880)

Granddaughter, I have returned as I promised. Quietly come with me. Tonight I want to tell you more about my daughter Maggie and the family.

In 1880 Maggie turned 17. She was living at home and working as a servant, but her life was about to change. It was hard to believe that my little daughter had grown into this beautiful woman with long, dark-brown, wavy hair, and greenish-golden eyes. She was smart, gracious, and well mannered. The excitement of first love was beaming from her young face, as she smiled at everyone and anything, even to the grumpy old man who lived across the street. She had ignored him until now, and he looked surprised as he turned to go back into his house.

Maggie always helped me around the house—cleaning, cooking, and caring for her brothers and sister. After five years of married life with Ben, we now had four-year-old Little Mary and two-year-old Albert.

I had learned many things from Maggie, partly because she was able to read to me and tell me things that were happening all around the world. In a way she also gave me back my hearing that was taken from me so many years before: I could read her lips, making it easier for me to communicate with others.

Maggie was a sensitive girl, and she was always quick to

find nice words that made us all feel good about ourselves. She would say, 'My brother Daniel is the finest gardener ever.'

She was right. Daniel spent his summers sitting in the garden, picking every blade of grass, carefully removing unwanted bugs and clipping off the wilted leaves. He grew gladiolas, irises, tulips, daffodils, lilies of the valley, daisies, sunflowers, and many other flowers. To me, the garden looked like a place that could have dropped down through the sky from Heaven.

Maggie also told everyone that her father was the hardest worker in town. And she bragged about my delicious, mouth-watering soups. What troubled her, though, was the teasing her brother received from other children around town. As Mrs. Jones had said, Daniel was teased because of his dark skin. But the boys also made fun of him because he limped.

Daniel had fallen from the porch and hurt his leg just after I married Ben. A neighbor had cut down two hornets' nests from his tree, and a swarm of hornets flew into our yard stinging Daniel. To protect himself, Daniel covered his head with his arms, blocking his eyes, so he could not see. Hornets attacking him, he screamed from the stings all over his body. The stingers also went right through his pants. He tumbled from the top porch step, yelling for help. I was in the house and did not hear him, but I just knew, Granddaughter—I cannot explain it—that something was wrong, and I walked to the front door to look out. There was Daniel lying on the ground.

I ran out, swatting the hornets away and fanning the air with my apron. I picked Daniel up and carried him back inside. I washed him and put wet cloth on his stings. His swollen right leg had cuts and bruises and he kept holding it and crying. I left him alone in the house and went for Ben at the station.

I rarely went there, but I needed him to come home. Ben knew that one of our neighbors, Mr. Bresser, had been a surgeon in the Civil War, when he lived in Maryland. We were lucky because Mr. Bresser was home. I ran ahead to be with Daniel, while Ben and our neighbor found two boards.

The men arrived a little later; Ben was out of breath. Mr. Bresser put one board on each side of Daniel's broken leg, wrapping cloth around the boards to make sure they did not move. He told us to keep the boards on Daniel's leg for a couple of months until it healed. When the boards were taken off, Daniel's leg was very stiff and he had a hard time walking from that day on.

Maggie and I would get so upset when we saw the mean neighborhood boys limp back and forth past our house, laughing. They would even throw rocks at my sweet boy when he was sitting in the garden. Maggie would run out to chase them away. Daniel would tell us not to worry. He said that it was okay and it did not bother him so much. He would tell us that those boys just did not have good mothers to teach them to be kind. Maggie would give Daniel a hug and say that she wished that the other boys could be half as good as her brother.

There I go again, Granddaughter, with my wandering memories. Now I will get back to my story about Maggie.

 **Sam**

Maggie met Samuel H. Tiberghien at the house where she worked as a servant. She was talking to another servant in the kitchen when a young man came to the back door to deliver a message. It turned out that the young man was the other servant's son. He came by to tell his mother that his aunt and uncle would be visiting at the end of the week.

Maggie noticed that he was very handsome when they were introduced. He continued talking to Maggie for quite a while, as she dusted the furniture, before he turned around to leave. Maggie told me that he even made the weather sound interesting.

She was so excited that she asked Sam's mother many questions about him. When Maggie came home that night, she talked to me all evening about him. She said that she wished I could have seen him standing there in his dark pants and blue shirt. He had dark hair and blue eyes. 'Sam, Sam, Sam' was all her lips could say.

She told me that his mother said that he was a billposter. I did not know what that was, so she explained that he hung advertisements so people could know things like when the circus was coming to town or where a big new store was located.

The next day at work Maggie learned that Sam had asked a hundred questions about her. Sam's mother said that her son wanted to know everything he could about Maggie. Before Maggie and Sam's mother finished talking, Sam stopped by to ask Maggie out. It was her first date. A few years earlier Sam had lost his young wife in an accident. And now he lived alone in an apartment downtown.

Sam asked Maggie to go with him to a concert. They went to several concerts before Maggie invited him over to meet us. He stayed for dinner a couple of times. He could not stop smiling or looking at my daughter. It was not long till he had a talk with Ben out in the backyard to ask permission to propose to Maggie. Ben told him that he would talk with me and let him know the next day.

Granddaughter, I did not want to see my Maggie go. I did not want anything to change. But I also wanted my daughter to be happy. I am sure that my mother wanted all the same things for me that I wanted for my girl. I hoped that Sam would be good to her and that he would love, protect, and provide for her. I hoped that he would take care of her gentle, kind spirit and make her happy. It was hard for me to let her go, but I knew that it was her decision and her time in life to be a woman. The next day Ben told Sam that it was okay with us for him to ask her. That night he did ask and she said 'Yes.'

After Sam left that evening, Ben took the children for a walk to the train overpass so that I could spend some time alone with Maggie. I sat with her in the garden and talked with her about being a wife. I told her that not all men treat women the same and that sometimes she might have to stand up for herself, even against her husband. I talked to her about the things that a man and wife do together when they are alone. I also told her about having babies. These were things that I had to learn pretty much on my own. I hoped that she would benefit from my experience.

She said that she was relieved that she had me to talk with because there were some things that she had been wondering about. She told me that I had answered many of her questions that she just did not know how to ask. I told her that she and Sam would have to be patient at first but in time they would enjoy their precious moments alone very much.

She asked me to help make her wedding dress and we started to work on it the next day. I was glad that I had saved a little money in a jar on top of the kitchen cupboard. I worked many hours on the wedding dress. The pins and needles left marks on my fingers and my eyes would start tearing after a while, but I just could not put it down.

Maggie helped in the evenings after work when she was not with Sam. It took only a few days to finish. As she tried on the dress, Maggie told me that she never knew that love could feel so good and she wanted to spend the rest of her life with Sam.

It was by far the most beautiful, delicate dress that either of us had ever seen. I added tiny white beads around the neckline and at the top of the long sleeves that were pleated at the shoulder.

Maggie loved those sleeves, which were full at the top and narrow at the wrist. There was a small slit at each wrist and a pearl button above the slit. But what she loved most was the skirt of the dress, which was covered in thin white lace with a line of beads sewn in the shape of miniature flowers along the bottom edge. A shiny silk band was tied around her small waist.

Maggie went shopping for a new pair of shoes. She was about 5 feet tall, like me, but her feet were much smaller than mine, and I did not know whether she would be able to find dress shoes small enough to fit her. But she came home with a beautiful pair of white shoes that matched the dress.

Daniel wanted to do something for Maggie, so he decided to make her a bouquet from his garden on the day of the wedding. Maggie tied the flowers together with a long white ribbon and saved a few small flowers to place in her hair. I would not allow the tears to come as I looked at this beautiful bride. My daughter, my firstborn, was getting married. Granddaughter, if only you could have seen her: the dress, the tiny white lily-of-the-valley flowers in her hair, and the glow on her pinkish cheeks. I felt so proud.

A preacher who Maggie and Sam chose stopped by our house to perform the wedding in the garden. Granddaughter, this was one of many times that I was sorry that I had lost my people's customs. If I remembered what Mother had taught me about the Supreme Creator, I could have taught my children more. I had learned a few things about the White Man's religion from Mrs. Carol when I was at the Friends home, but it just was not the same as knowing our own Indian wedding traditions.

Sam, a few friends, and the family waited outside until Maggie was ready. Ben came in to walk with her to the garden. My baby girl put her hand into Sam's. Sam then slid a shiny gold band onto Maggie's finger and kissed her. We sat for a short time in the garden and had something to eat. I could not hold back my tears any longer after our guests left, and I walked back inside my home without my daughter. Ben kept the other children outside for a while to give me a little time.

The ceremony took only minutes, but our lives were changed forever.

Maternal Lineage:
Maggie Cox Tiberghien

2nd Great - grandmother	First Husband	Year Married	Children
Maggie Cox (1863-1913)	Sam Tiberghien (1849-1896)	1880	Sammy Jr. (1881-1883)
			William (1883-1918)
			Ida (1885-1961)
			Twins (1886-1886)
			Belle (1887-1960)
			George (1888-1959)
			Charles (1889-1959)
			Willard (1890-unknown)
			Twins (1891-1891)
			Amelia (1893-1982)
			Mary (1894-1897)
			Bertha (1895-1897)

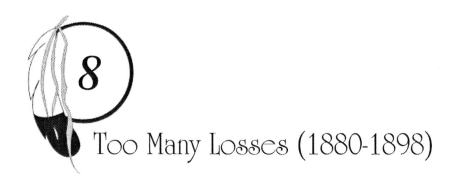

Too Many Losses (1880-1898)

Maggie and Sam were ready to start a family. And after their first month as husband and wife, Maggie became pregnant and gave birth to Sammy Jr. in 1881.

Sammy Jr. was a joy, but he cried much of the time and would not eat right. He had to be encouraged to take milk and then would spit it up. He was always sick with a fever and a cough. Scarlet fever took him on August 15, 1883, when he was only one year and eight months old. He was buried in Spring Grove Cemetery in a plain wooden box, just like the one that held my two poor babies.

Maggie was very sad when she lost Sammy Jr., so I stayed with her for a couple of weeks. She would cry and stay in bed, not having the strength to get up. I told her that she had to take care of herself and the second child she was expecting. I helped Maggie brush her beautiful long hair that reached her shoulders. Sometimes she wore it in a bun, just to get it out of her way. But Sam liked when she wore it loose.

She gave birth to a baby boy on August 31, 1883 and named him William after my father. This was just two weeks after Sammy was buried. I continued staying with Maggie, trying to comfort her. I felt her pain, but I had to be strong for her. When I was certain that Maggie could go on, I went home and grieved for my own boy Albert, who had passed away a few months earlier. Up to that point, I had just never allowed myself time to cry.

Albert was four years old when he was trampled by a runaway horse. Granddaughter, it was really my fault. I did not notice him when he woke up from his morning nap because I was washing clothes in the kitchen. He went out the front door and walked into the street. I had told him so many times not to go into the street. Why did he not listen?

While Daniel was working in the garden, he heard a crash and saw a horse running wild. He saw young Albert lying in the street. Daniel quickly came through the front door, panting and stumbling. He kept stomping his feet, so I could hear him. I knew something was wrong when I saw his face, eyes, and mouth wide open. Looking out the window, I froze, hardly able to move. It was like the way I felt right after my childhood accident, but worse.

Someone at the train station also saw the accident and told Ben that a child was hurt in front of our home. Ben came rushing up the street screaming when he saw the child was his son. When Ben arrived at Albert's side, he started chanting and singing in his native language on his knees in the street. I could not hear him but I knew exactly what he was doing. He was praying, with open hands high in the air, for his son to be taken to a good place where Ben's mother was.

Ben had been so hurt when Albert passed away that I had to concentrate on taking care of my husband as well as Little Mary, who was now six. The day of the accident was the first time I ever saw Ben cry. Seeing him like that worried me that Ben would not be able to stop. I was afraid for Little Mary and Daniel, too. I did not know what to expect. But I knew that I could not show my own feelings because my family needed me to guard them and not think of my own pain. I asked Ben to carry Albert into the house, away from the group of people who were gathering in front of our home to see what had happened. In time our life slowly returned to normal, although not seeing Albert's smiling face was almost unbearable. I could see that Ben was glad that we still had two children at home. Ben would walk around the backyard with Little Mary on his back and Daniel at his side as he made up some kind of story or just repeated one of their old favorites. Little Mary was starting to make up little stories of her own. She had such a good imagination, and her father had been a good teacher.

About this time Daniel worked for the Taft family, a political family living in Indian Hills, not too far from Madeira. Mr. Taft's son once stopped by our place, saying that our garden was the best in town. As Mr. Taft stood in our backyard looking around, he hired Daniel on the spot and they shook hands. Daniel cared for the Taft gardens, and Mr. Taft said that Daniel had the gift of gardening.

We all felt so proud. After Mr. Taft left, Daniel came to me and told me not to worry because he would keep our garden just as nice as always. He knew how much I loved his flowers and vegetables. He said that he would always have beautiful flowers for me. Granddaughter, he was such a good son.

Maggie, Sam, and William lived in downtown Cincinnati. Even though William seemed small for his age, he was much happier and healthier than Sammy Jr. Maggie worried about living so close to town with him because he might get sick like her first baby. She worried about the river flooding and about strange people living there. Maggie had reason to worry because of the record floods in 1883 and 1884. There was also rioting in town. Maggie could hear all the noise, so she stayed inside with her son.

There was much anger about the sentence in a murder trial. A man was convicted of killing his boss, the livery-stable owner. The murderer's punishment was 20 years in prison for manslaughter. Thousands of rioters wanted to hang the murderer, but they were stopped by the National Guard, militia, and Gatling guns. The rioters burned down the courthouse, and they destroyed the Cincinnati Law Library, with many records lost.

I remember when Maggie came to the house and told me about the events. But she was even more concerned about the threat of her child being taken away. She had read in the newspaper that Indian children were being taken from their families to live in boarding schools. She decided that the only way to keep her boy safe was not to tell him about our Indian background.

I felt sad because I wanted to share my stories about my mother with my grandchildren just as I had told my own children, but I understood that we had to keep William safe. I did not want anyone to take any of our children away from us. I would have to keep a good eye on my Little Mary with her dark skin and Indian features. My Maggie and her son William had much lighter skin, and people could easily think that they were both white.

Granddaughter, why would the White Man want to do this to us? Did he not have enough children? Why take ours? I wondered whether there would ever be an end to what the White Man wanted. I was not going to let anyone take my children away. I was going to do whatever I had to do for them. In time I worried less, but the possibility of trouble was always in the back of my mind.

Life for Ben, Daniel, Little Mary, and me was pretty quiet at our home. Ben and Daniel fished several times a week in fair weather down by the train overpass. We all liked eating their fresh catches plus the rabbits, squirrels, and turtles that they brought home. Daniel and Marry liked to pick wild berries or cherries in season for me to make pies.

On their way walking home, Little Mary would take one of the berries, smash it, and color her cheeks, nose, and lips. When I saw her painted face, I would laugh, and she would smile. She knew how much we missed Albert and she tried to take away some of our sorrow by being cute or funny. She was such a joy to all of us.

In the summer of 1885, Maggie told us that she was expecting another baby. She told me she was wishing for a girl, and her wish came true when Ida Mary was born on December 20, 1885. She was called Ida because we had Little Mary, and we did not want the children to become confused.

Maggie came to visit every week with her son and daughter. That winter Daniel made a sled to pull Little Mary and William around in the snow. In the spring William played in the garden with his aunt and uncle, Little Mary and Daniel. The children loved being out there together, chasing after bugs and playing ball. Maggie and I enjoyed time with Baby Ida in the kitchen while we cooked or sewed. In the summer Maggie helped Daniel weed the garden, while Little Mary and I watched the two babies.

◆◆◆◆◆◆◆ Little Mary ◆◆◆◆◆◆◆

Later that summer, Little Mary had a fever. I tried to take care of her, but I did not know what was wrong. As she limped on her way to the privy, I noticed a sore on the bottom of her foot and several reddish lines going up the back of her leg. I thought she must have gotten a splinter from the porch. She never liked to tell me when she got a splinter or cut because she did not want anyone to touch it. She would try to hide any wound.

When Maggie came over later that day, she and I took Little Mary to the town doctor. Although she was ten years old, I carried her all the way, a thin blanket wrapped around her body and her warm head against my neck. Ben and Daniel kept Maggie's two children at our house. The doctor had a small office in the downstairs of his home. He said that Little Mary had been bitten or maybe she had stepped on something and had a bad infection.

Little Mary never told us how she got that sore on her foot. Maybe she did not know. The doctor opened the sore with a small knife, squeezed her foot, and thick yellowish liquid dripped out. I could feel Little Mary moan and sniff all the way home and then she fell asleep.

I did everything the doctor said to do for her; I did not want her to lose her foot. Maggie could not stay to help me because she had to return home with her two children. Little Mary grew worse and started talking out of her head during the night. She just stopped breathing and passed away early in the morning the next day. I stayed at her side all night. She reached out for my hand, looked up at me, and I saw her lips in the dim, flickering lamplight as she said, 'I love you, Mama.' I told her that I loved her with a heart like the Blue Mountain and she quietly closed her eyes in peace.

Her little doll, which I had made years earlier, was lying in the crease of her arm. She was wearing her nightgown and cap. A soft blanket covered her small body. I looked around the room where I could see her toys. Her pictures that she had drawn were hanging on the walls. I wrapped the blanket around her and carried Little Mary outside to the garden and sat in my wooden chair with her all that morning. I sang mother's song to her over and over. *Oh Ho Oh Ho Shaya holta.* . . . I was glad that I had taught it to her.

While I sat in the garden, I remembered watching my youngest sing along with me. Granddaughter, I had never heard a single sound from her lips but I knew her footsteps on the floor, the smell of her hair and body, the love in her heart, the laughter from her spirit, and the look in her eye when she wanted something. I knew everything there was to know about her. I knew her like no other person knew her. She was my sweet baby girl who came from inside my own body. I was the one she depended on and now she was gone.

As I sat outside, cradling her body, I continued talking to Little Mary, telling her about my mother who loved us. I told her about my childhood and how when I was about five years old, my father thought it would be fun to tell me that I could ride a deer if I could catch one. He said for me to walk up slowly and quietly and jump on the deer's back. He told me to wrap my arms around her neck and my legs around her belly so I would not fall off.

Years later Father said that when he saw me walk up to the deer without their being frightened, Father was the one who became frightened that the animals would hurt me. But I would quietly say: It is okay. It is okay. It is okay. I will not hurt you, as I softly waved my hands through the air as though I were stroking their backs. The deer would tilt their heads and just look at me wondering what I was doing. And then they would run off.

Then I realized that my youngest daughter had just done the same thing as the deer. She slipped off, leaving me there alone. I cried. I knew that she was gone and I would never see her smiling face again. She would never do her funny little things to make me laugh. I even thought for a while on asking my mother again to take me to be with her, but I knew that it would be wrong to leave Ben, Daniel, and the others.

Ben had to help me this time. He had to persuade me that it was time to let her go. After Little Mary was buried, Ben grew very quiet. He was never the same after that day. It was as though he aged 20 years overnight. Ben walked more slowly as he went to work. He even started walking with a limp because his knees, back, and hips started bothering him. He often rubbed his stiff hands.

He stopped telling his stories and did not talk much. He lost most of his appetite and just wanted to sit in the garden, his straw hat pulled down low, leaning back in his old wooden chair. His naps started lasting longer.

As I looked out at him from the back kitchen door, I could sometimes see his lips moving, but I never knew what he was saying or who he was saying it to. I thought maybe he was still talking to the children the same way I still talked to my mother.

I had to find strength deep inside myself. Believing it came from my mother, it helped me get up each day, eat, and do the things that I needed to do. Each of us has that strength inside. Granddaughter, we just have to find it when we need it. I learned how very thankful I was for the people I loved and for each day that I had with them. I also learned that life is full of constant change and I had to accept the things that I had no power over. I would never stop missing my baby girl, but I had to concentrate on life and those I could help.

 **More Babies**

Just before Ida was a year old, Maggie had twins. They were two tiny girls with dark hair. They both had difficulty breathing and passed away just after birth. Maggie did not even name them. She just referred to them as the twins. They were dressed alike and buried in the same box.

In October of 1887 Maggie gave birth to Margaret Belle, who was named after her mother. We called the baby Belle. In November 1888 George Albert came along. His middle name was the same as my passed-on son's name. His brother Charles was born on August 5, 1889, and another brother Willard, in 1890.

Maggie lost another set of twins in the winter of 1891, when she had a very bad cold early in her pregnancy. Her harsh coughing all night affected the twins' development, and they looked more like two little 6-inch sea horses than babies. Maggie wept as she showed them to me, as we told them good-bye. Daniel made a nice little wooden box for them. Maggie wrapped them together in a small blanket and we buried them in the garden.

Maggie had another baby girl, Mary Amelia, who was born on April 10, 1893. She had lots of dark curly hair. Named after my daughter Little Mary, she was called Amelia. Another baby girl, just named Mary, was born to Maggie and Sam the next year. Maggie did not give her a middle name because she wanted her to be called Mary. Bertha Elizabeth was born in March of 1895. She was named after my Elizabeth, who passed before she was even a year old.

Maggie had 14 babies in 15 years. William, Ida, Belle, George, Charles, Willard, Amelia, Mary and Bertha were the nine children still with her. Sammy Jr. was buried in Spring Grove Cemetery, and the two sets of tiny twins were quietly placed in our garden among Daniel's flower beds.

◆◆◆◆◆◆◆ Sam's Misfortune ◆◆◆◆◆◆◆

Sam had gone to work early on a cool September morn. He worked all day but did not come home. Working late was not unusual, so Maggie did not think much of it, even though she did not like it. Sometimes on payday he would go for a drink after work with his friends.

Later that evening Barney, Sam's best friend who worked with Sam, came by Maggie's home to tell her that her husband was in the hospital. She asked a neighbor to keep an eye on the children, as she rushed to see what had happened. Sam passed away before she arrived. The doctor would not let her in to see the body. He told Maggie that Sam had many cuts, broken bones, and injuries and that an investigation was about to start.

Maggie never really got to the truth of what had happened

to her husband and none of his work buddies would talk about it. They said that all they knew was that he had had an accident. They told Maggie that they heard Sam moaning and found him bleeding in the alleyway behind the billposter office. When he would not open his eyes or talk to them, they took him to Cincinnati Hospital.

Sam was only 47 when he passed away. He was buried in Spring Grove Cemetery. I kept the little ones at my house while Maggie went to the burial. She rode the train back to our house to spend a night before going home. She was so exhausted that she just fell asleep in her black dress and shoes until one of the babies woke her during the night for milk.

Maggie knew that she could not raise all her children in our small house, so she looked for a job in order to pay the rent, handle the bills, and buy food. She got a job in a meatpacking factory, even though it was a distance to walk every morning and evening.

She had to walk about a half-hour each way in good weather. The factory paid a little better than some of the other local factories and businesses. But the workdays were long, hot, and smelly. The work bothered her so much that she could no longer eat meat.

When William was 13, he found a job at an old dairy farm, shoveling manure out of the barns, carrying hay, and pumping water. Ida quit school to care for the four little ones: Willard, Amelia, Mary, and Bertha. Belle, George, and Charles went to school.

The winter was hard, but somehow Maggie and her children made it through. That was until the children caught colds in February. The two youngest, Mary and Bertha, were still sick in March, when they developed bronchitis. Maggie found Mary cold and still one morning, and a couple of days later she found Bertha the same way. It was three days before Bertha's 2nd birthday.

Maggie's boss yelled at her for missing work that week, even though he knew about her children. After she begged for her job, he said that he would give her just one more chance. We did not see much of Maggie during this time because she was working so much. Daniel was working, too, but he made trips over to Maggie's to check on her children as often as he could and took food and other things that they needed.

I was sad to see Maggie and her babies struggling to survive. We tried to help them as much as we could. We added a few rows to our vegetable garden to have more food to share with Maggie and the children, I helped make clothes for them, and Daniel gave part of his paycheck to help with their rent. Ben and I could not give much money to Maggie because Ben was getting older and could not work as many hours as before.

Ben's health was not as good as when he was younger. Sometimes he would come down with a bad cough that would take a long time to go away. He was starting to drink medicine from a flask because it helped him sleep at night. Sometimes he filled in at the station by doing cleanup jobs. A younger, faster man was hired to do most of the work that Ben had done before turning 70.

The children took turns staying at our house, so I could watch them. I cut their hair and saw that they got a good scrubbing. Granddaughter, there is nothing as sweet as the smell of children who have just bathed. Fresh and clean and pure, they remind me of my childhood and the cool creek waters where my mother used to bathe me.

The children would sit in a washtub on the floor and soak clean down to their little nails. Adding some coal to the stove to warm the kitchen and hanging blankets over chairs around the tub would cut down on any winter drafts.

I also washed and sewed the children's clothes when they needed mending. I liked to hang them outside to dry so they smelled fresh, but if the weather was freezing, I hung a clothesline in the kitchen. When the children were sick, we helped care for them, too. They were always on my mind and in my heart.

Maternal Lineage:
Maggie Cox Tiberghien Stapleton

2nd Great - grandmother	Second Husband	Year Married	Children
Maggie Cox Tiberghien (1863-1913)	Enyard Stapleton (1864-1915)	1898	Scott (1899-1964)
			James (1901-1922)
			Mary (1902-1904)
			Twins (1904-1904)

9

Great Tribulations (1898-1915)

Maggie was fired from her job when she sprained her ankle, walking home from work. She was looking up into the dark, cloudy sky, wondering whether she could make it home before the rain started again. The wind was blowing and leaves were falling from the trees. She did not see the muddy hole in her path until she was sitting in it. The next morning she bound her ankle and tried to work, but it hurt too much and she could not pay attention to what she was doing.

It did not take long for the boss to notice her limping, so he sent her home. He was upset with her because she had missed work when the babies were so sick a few weeks earlier. Now with a sprained ankle, she would be missing more work. He fired Maggie, telling her that he could find someone else to do the job who did not have so many 'woman problems.' He said that she got hurt too easily, had too many children, and needed to find a husband so she could stay home.

Maggie stayed home for several weeks until her leg was better. We brought the youngest children to our house, and 12-year-old Ida helped her mother. As soon as she could, Maggie found another job at an overalls factory. She said that sewing was much better than working at the stinky meat plant. Even though her hands were always callused and chapped from all the work she did at home, she needed the factory job and could not complain that her fingers hurt.

It was also cold during the winter in the sewing room. Maggie wore the special gloves I knitted for her, the ones that did not cover her fingers. I thought they would keep her hands a little warmer and she could still sew.

She told me what happened when her boss saw her wearing the gloves: Maggie said that they were not allowed because they would prevent her from sewing properly. She told her boss that she had to wear them because she would not be able to move her cold hands. He yelled at her and said that she had to get rid of them or she could leave. She took them off and put them in her pocket, continuing to work.

The next part of her story always made me laugh. As her boss turned to walk away, Maggie poked her finger under her nose to lift it up at him for thinking he was so much better than she was, but as soon as she did it, she quickly put her hand down and looked around the room to make sure that no one had noticed her. She did not want to lose this job, even if her boss was unreasonable, hard, and uncaring.

◆◆◆◆◆◆ Desperation ◆◆◆◆◆◆

On Maggie's first week at her new job, she met Enyard Stapleton, who was her age. Towering over her, he had hazel eyes and medium brown hair. He worked at another factory next door to where Maggie worked. When they left work at the same time, they walked in the same direction. Enyard caught up to her and asked whether she was new because he had not seen her before. She nodded yes.

They saw each other over the next few days and would smile or wave. Enyard would say, 'Hello, Green Eyes.' By the end of the week, he asked Maggie her name and she asked him his. The next Monday, he waited for her outside the factory door after work and asked whether she was single. She told him that her husband had passed away.

Enyard asked her to go out. She told him that she could not because she had to get home to her children. He asked whether he could meet them. She invited him to her home the next Sunday, giving him her address. He came all dressed up, holding a box of chocolates for Maggie and a bag of black licorice for the children. Maggie told me that his eyes and mouth opened wide when he saw six children, age 12 all the way down to four. But Enyard had a nice day playing ball and tag in the backyard while getting to know the children and Maggie.

William was not living at home any longer. He had just moved into a small room next to the barn where he worked. It saved him from traveling back and forth every day. He was still helping Maggie with a little grocery money.

Enyard made plans to come back the next Sunday. On that visit he brought a cake and some bread that his mother had baked just for Maggie. Maggie and Enyard learned from each other that their mothers were both named Mary Ann.

It was not long before Enyard asked Maggie to marry him. He told her that he had been engaged, but his fiancée kept putting off the wedding date, so Enyard and the girl called off the engagement. Maggie was a little worried because she had not known Enyard for long, but she agreed in hopes of a better life, especially for her children.

Maggie and Enyard had a very quiet wedding in the courthouse, each inviting one friend to be a witness. Enyard helped Maggie and the children move into his wood-framed farmhouse just on the edge of town. Built shortly after the end of the Civil War, the 32-year-old home sheltered three generations of Enyard's family, with his mother still living there. It was larger than Maggie's and there was a nice yard for the children. His pencil drawings of animals, trees, and buildings hung on the walls.

The happiness during dating disappeared once Maggie married Enyard. He tried to control Maggie, who had to put her own feelings aside, doing things just to keep him calm and quiet so he would not storm out of the house and return late in the evening as he would do quite often if he did not get his way. Enyard also controlled his wife's time. He told her that she did not need to see her girlfriend anymore. Maggie had only one friend because Maggie was always so busy with the children and work. She felt terrible as she pushed her friend away to avoid problems at home.

Constantly bragging about everything he had ever done, Enyard had a way of showing off as if he were better and smarter than everyone else. His mother and Maggie made excuses for him, and he did not even know that most people just tolerated him. But I will have to say, Granddaughter, that sometimes when he was in a good mood, he was funny and made everyone laugh. He was also handy with tools. And he was a talented artist. He had a big drawing tablet full of doodles and other pencil drawings. But he never really put that gift to much use.

Enyard's lack of self-control affected the children, but not as much as it did Maggie. She tried to protect them from Enyard's anger and outbursts. The children spent much time outdoors, playing and out of his way.

Enyard had a chicken coop in the backyard, and a big black-and-white striped rooster named Doodle Do ruled the roost. The rooster liked to chase the children when they went to the outhouse. Charles, Willard, and Amelia would run and squeal with the rooster, the bird pecking at their heels. A couple of times the rooster was found down the hole when someone left the door open to the privy. No one knew how or why he got down there, but they would put a long branch down for him to climb out. Once free, Doodle Do would be in a bad mood for a couple of days, and everyone knew to give him plenty of space.

One day a big old shaggy, floppy-eared dog followed Ida and Belle home from the store. George named him *Old Itchy Buns* and soon everyone knew why. The younger children would laugh until they fell down when they saw *Old Itchy Buns* walking on two front legs and dragging his bottom around with his hind legs stretched out ahead. He walked this way so much that he wore the hair off. A couple of weeks later he disappeared—not to be seen again. The children looked for him with no luck. Enyard said that he must have worn himself down to nothing.

Enyard also brought a black cat home one time. He thought it would help cut down on mice. He had found the cat climbing through the garbage pile and named him *Crummy*. At least the children did not have to worry about feeding their new pet because *Crummy* knew how to find his own food. Even so, George made sure that *Crummy* always had water in a small old lunch bucket that he had left by the back door for the cat to drink.

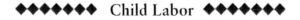

◆◆◆◆◆◆◆ Child Labor ◆◆◆◆◆◆◆

Maggie was expecting another baby, and Enyard would not let her work anymore. So when Belle turned 12 years old, she had to quit school to go to work. Enyard insisted that Belle was old enough to get a job at the shirt factory, which was close enough for her to walk to work. He told Belle to say that she was 14, so she would be hired because there were some rules about hiring younger children. Enyard went with her on the first day. Even though she was short for her age, she said that she was 14. The supervisor looked up at Enyard, who nodded his head. No more proof was required

Before leaving, Enyard told Belle, shaking his finger in her face, that she better not mess up because it was her responsibility to help support her brothers and sisters. Belle listened.

Working conditions were not good. The overseer was constantly watching and yelling about any mistakes that workers made, which were deducted from their pay. If workers were late, not fast enough, or not able to do the work, they were replaced and sent home. Belle worked hard because she needed this job.

Her small pay did not go far. For her first two months, she spent her paycheck to buy badly needed shoes for the rest of the children, one pair at a time. Then she bought heavy material for me to make coats for them for the winter. Each payday Belle bought two sweet rolls on her way home for the children to share that night after dinner.

All the children would be waiting outside for her to come home on payday, but Amelia would watch and wait for Belle every day. They were very close. Ida was close with Belle, too, but she was usually busy helping with the boys, folding laundry from the clothesline or helping her mother prepare dinner.

Maggie and Enyard had a son Scott in 1899. In 1901 James was born. Both boys looked just like their father. In 1902 Maggie gave birth to a daughter she named Mary, who looked just like Maggie, with her green eyes and wavy-brown hair and dainty features.

Maggie had trouble through all these pregnancies, and she did not have much help. Enyard's mother was not well and could not help much with the young ones, even though she lived in the house. She was happy when Enyard told her that the baby girl Mary was named after her. So now, Granddaughter, we had another Mary in our family.

After Mary was born, Belle turned 16. Enyard was hard on Belle, pushing her to clean and care for the children in addition to working full time. Belle once told me that he was never happy with what she did, even when she tried to please him for her mother's sake. Maggie was upset that her daughter was mistreated, but Enyard would just yell at his wife, saying that she was babying Belle. With no strength to stand up to him, Maggie gave in.

Belle finally told her mother that it was impossible to continue living at home. Maggie was heartbroken when Belle moved in with a well-to-do family and became the nanny. But Belle lived close by, so she and her mother could visit when Enyard was not at home.

◆◆◆◆◆◆ Sad Good-Byes ◆◆◆◆◆◆

Maggie was sad with her daughter's decision, but Maggie had her own problems, and the following year she was pregnant again. Two-year-old Mary was very sick, breaking out in a rash on her face and arms. At first Maggie thought it was from the heat, but then Baby Mary's beautiful hair started to fall out and she would not eat. My poor Maggie could not enjoy the birth of her third set of twins, who were born about this time. About two weeks after their birth, they had passed on, and Maggie buried them and Baby Mary, who just did not have a chance. Maggie was brokenhearted, but she and Enyard were both having health problems of their own.

Several months earlier, Enyard had a couple of wet sores on his face and arms, and the next month Maggie had the same thing. The sores cleared up, and then she started being bothered by bad headaches and nausea. Enyard was not well, but Maggie was worse because she was still weak from her last pregnancy.

When Baby Mary and the twins passed away, the medical examiner determined that they died from syphilis. He said that Baby Mary could have been infected from Enyard's rash that continued to ooze on his arms. And the twins had definitely gotten the sickness through Maggie's blood before they were born.

Maggie was crushed when Enyard admitted to the examiner that he had been spending time with some girls who hung out downtown. Enyard said that he had no idea that he caught any disease. Granddaughter, can you imagine the heartbreak? I was sick with the news. The babies were gone, and their parents were well into the second stage of syphilis.

Amelia, Scott, and James were only 11, 5, and 3 when Maggie sent them by train to stay with me and Ben. In a short time, my Maggie grew more tired and she lost weight. She had problems swallowing and her knees swelled, making it difficult for her to walk. She also had a slight fever. When her mind was affected, she was taken to Longview Hospital. There was no cure for this terrible disease, and many people died from it, some not even knowing what they had.

While Maggie was in the hospital, Belle met Wilbert Hall, who had come from Detroit to Cincinnati on business and stopped by the home where Belle was working. She was so taken by Wilbert.

Handsome, with dark-brown, curly hair and blue eyes, he stood about 5 feet, 9 inches, and he walked with a swing in his step as if he were listening to music. Belle told me that his lively walk attracted her to him because she loved to dance. Like Belle, he was outgoing, talking to everyone he met. But looks can fool people because he was very stubborn, always wanting to get his way.

Wilbert liked Belle, too, and asked her to come to see him in Detroit. He had given her directions on how to find him if she ever wanted to come for a visit. Deciding that she needed a change, she took a train to find him.

It was hard for me to sleep with so many thoughts going

through my mind, but when I would fall asleep I had my dreams. Often I saw my parents.

One morning, I awoke suddenly after a dream in which I was listening to my father. He was telling me that my mother's parents sometimes called my mother their *Wechumpe, like the stars.* He told me that we see the stars only at night, but they are there all the time. The sun is just too bright for us to see the stars in the day. He told me that even though I could not see Mother, she was still with me just like the stars and then he walked away. I was thankful to know that my mother was still there with me.

I realized then that Father had passed on for sure because only those who passed on came to me in my dreams. As I awoke, I thought about my loving daughter and how much I already missed her beautiful smile.

Maggie continued to suffer until 1913, when she passed away in her hospital room alone. We were not even allowed to visit her. I wish that I had known when it was our last time together, so I could have told her good-bye.

I believe that she was afraid and confused. She was only 50 when she passed, and sick for her last nine years. Unable to be with her family and the children she loved, she even had grandchildren before she passed away, but, sadly, she did not know them. Her own children were told that she died from mental illness caused by change of life because the doctor did not think it was wise to tell them the truth.

If I had known that I would not see her again, I would have held onto her a little tighter and a little longer and kissed her face, telling her what she meant to me, how wonderful she was, and how very much I loved her. I would have given her flowers or a warm blanket or something to show that I cared.

I would have taken Maggie's place, Granddaughter, if I could. Many things went through my mind that I still wanted to do for her and with her, but she was gone. Her leaving was as big a change for me as when she had come into my life. Maggie and I had been so close that I did not know where I stopped and she started.

Enyard was having one trouble after another. His mother died from heart problems. He lost his job because he missed too many days of work because of his failing health; his boss told him not to come back. Enyard sold the house and lived in a tiny apartment.

He came by our house and picked up his two sons Scott and Jimmy, who were living with us. Enyard said that he missed the boys and wanted them to live with him. There was nothing that we could do about it. After Enyard left, I felt ill. His cigar smoke hung in the air, reminding me that the boys were not coming back. Once I baked some apples and opened all the windows, I started feeling a little better.

At least, I was glad that he left Amelia with me. As a young teen, she needed a woman to care for her. Granddaughter, Amelia told me everything that was on her mind. She would tell me how she always wanted to have thin, straight hair like Belle's instead of thick curly hair. I told her that her sister always wanted curly hair.

It was tough for Maggie's children because no one can take the place of a mother. And their father was not very helpful. He had a habit of making excuses, blaming everyone else for his problems. We also learned from Maggie, years before she passed, that some of Enyard's friends were real trouble. They drank too much and got violent. Two of them had been in jail when they were younger because they robbed a downtown store. Maggie did not trust them and argued with Enyard to stop seeing them, but he would not listen.

William had been living alone for some time. Ida had a

room at the home where she was working as a servant. George enlisted in the Army because he saw the service as a chance to better his life. Charles got a job and moved in with William. Willard had run away from home after Maggie got sick, and we never heard from him again nor did we learn where he went. He had always been a loner, but he did very well in school. So we prayed that his learning would help him.

Enyard was losing his mind from the disease. One night he was drinking at a bar and became loud. The owner just thought Enyard was drunk and threw him out the door. Enyard died after falling head first on the sidewalk; he had broken his neck.

When my neighbor told me that she read in the newspaper that Enyard had died, she, Daniel, and I went to Enyard's neighbors to find Scott and Jimmy. Someone said that the two boys had been taken to the House of Refuge just a short time after they went to live with their dad. Left home with nothing to eat, the boys had to steal, and finally someone reported them, and they were taken from their father. When we heard the news, we walked to the refuge to get the boys.

Walking into that building brought back horrible memories of the insane asylum, where I spent too many years. I just wanted to get out of there. We talked to a man, who sent a woman to get Jimmy, while the man said, 'Scott had run away.'

A few minutes later we saw a familiar face come into the room. Jimmy cried out, 'Grandma,' running to me and throwing his thin arms around. He held my arms down so I could not move, burying his head into my chest and not letting go. Jimmy could not talk for a while. Daniel said that when the boy did speak, his voice sounded deeper.

Jimmy was so glad to come home again. I fixed him a bed in the front room for the first couple of weeks. When I would wake up early in the mornings, I would find him sleeping on the floor in my room. He just wanted to feel close and safe, so I let him.

We later found his brother Scott, who had escaped from the House of Refuge and was living on the street. The five long hard years had taken a toll on both of their lives. They lived with us until they found jobs and a place to live on their own.

Granddaughter, Maggie and her babies caught this terrible disease just as if they had caught a cold. I believe that Maggie had no reason to be ashamed. She was a good daughter, wife, and mother. Knowing about her life may help someone else. Maggie would be glad for that.

It was wrong for the doctor to lie to the children about what happened to their mother. It was wrong for him to tell us not to say anything to them. I should have told them the truth, even though he said that it was best not to tell. I have learned that people can learn from the truth better than from lies.

I can only imagine how Maggie felt when she found out what had happened. Disease cut short the lives of three children plus my daughter and Enyard. It may have helped Maggie to know that I did not blame her. But it was too late. I wanted to tell her that I would do all I could for her children, but I am sure she knew.

There is much about life that a young woman does not understand, but some of it starts to become clearer as years go by. We do not always use our good senses about choices. I was lucky to have been with two good men. I also knew how to stand my ground and be strong. I learned my lessons the hard way, but I learned.

Maternal Lineage:
Belle Tiberghien Hall

1st Great - grandmother	First Husband	Year Married	Children
Belle Tiberghien (1887-1960)	Wilbert Hall (1886-1951)	1910	Margaret (1911-1992)
			Violet (1914-2002)
			Baby Son (1915-1915)
			Baby Son (1919-1919)
			Norma Ellen (1920-1920)

Coming Home
(1910-1924)

Granddaughter, I will now back up a couple of years to tell you about Belle, Maggie's daughter. You already know a little about Belle's difficult childhood. I cannot remember whether I told you, but she moved to Detroit before her mother passed away, leaving her family in Cincinnati. In 1910 Belle married Wilbert Hall at the justice of the peace. She was 23 and he was 24. After the ceremony they celebrated with Wilbert's friends.

I found out later that Wilbert had a very interesting life as a boy. The first of twin boys, he was born in the Canadian woodlands in the French province of Quebec. When he was born, Wilbert's mother was home alone because his dad was hunting elk with their older sons. Wilbert's mother thought that he was stillborn, so she lifted the child, wrapping him in a blanket, and put him into a firewood box that sat on the floor next to the stove. To her surprise, she started labor again and delivered her second son, Wilson, minutes later.

After caring for her newborn son and herself, she started a fire and cooked dinner for the family. That evening, when her husband and boys came home, she proudly showed them the new baby boy sleeping in his crib. She told her husband that there were two boys, but the first one passed over. Pointing to the wooden box, she asked her husband to bury the baby on the hill behind their cabin next to where their parents were buried.

When his father slid the box out and looked inside the box, he saw a slight movement of the baby's eyes under his lids and realized that Wilbert was alive. The heat from the stove had probably helped save him.

The twins spent their childhood in Canada hunting, fishing, and playing tough games with their older brothers. Usually doing things to get their older brothers into trouble, the twins were a handful, but their mother knew what they were up to. She was always disciplining them, without any help from their dad. He thought the twins were just being boys, and he would not help her. Instead he said that she should not be so hard on them.

The family moved to Detroit, Michigan, when the twins were 13 years old, buying a house just outside the downtown Detroit area, but the twins spent much of their time in town, up to no good. They would untie horses, letting them run wild, tease other children, peek in store windows, and annoy customers. The young twins even tried to enter a bar to buy drinks. Everyone knew the boys after a while and would just chase the pests away.

Finally realizing that he would have to work to support himself, Wilbert found a job at the Cadillac manufacturing plant, just before he met Belle. After he and Belle married, they lived close to the car company. And in 1911 Wilbert and Belle had their first baby, Margaret Amelia Hall. They called her Margaret.

Belle's sister Amelia left Madeira, where she was staying with me, and moved in with Belle and Wilbert to help with the baby. Belle's mother, Maggie, was in the hospital, unable to give any support to her daughters. Granddaughter, Belle had not seen her mother in a long time. And it was while expecting her second, daughter, Violet, that Belle learned of her own mother's death.

◆◆◆◆◆◆◆ Changing Times ◆◆◆◆◆◆◆

Life was changing very quickly. Silent movies had just come out, new dances were the latest craze, and fashions showed more of a woman's body, like their shoulders and ankles, unthinkable only a few years earlier.

The sisters enjoyed each other's company, and they tried to get out once in a while. The first silent film *Hello Broadway* was produced in 1913 and the two sisters went to see it. Good dancers, the girls tried the new, popular two-step and other dances.

Belle and Amelia visited me with Belle's two daughters a month or so after Violet was born in 1914. Belle and Amelia danced for me so I could see what all the fuss was about with the new music.

A few years later George and Charles, two of Belle's brothers, were fighting in Europe during the Great War. The boys sent letters, and George sent me picture postcards of the Mona Lisa and the Eiffel Tower, when he was in Paris. I asked my neighbor Melina, who also had two sons in the Army, to read my mail, so we both learned what was going on so far away. George would write about all the death and injuries, and he could not wait until he came home.

I found out later from Belle that life with Wilbert was not easy. He abused her and the children. He would drink too much and yell. When he was angry, he would hit Belle and the children. But he took out most of his anger on Belle, giving her a black eye several times. How he treated her, Granddaughter, made me angry and sad. But life continues, and Belle delivered two sons who were stillborn. In December 1920 Norma Ellen was born, but she lived only two days.

While Amelia was living at Belle's, she saw how her brother-in-law treated Belle and the children. At about that time,

Wilbert's nephew, Clarence, who would visit often, moved in, helping with the rent.

Amelia liked Clarence right away, seeing that he was not like his uncle at all. Clarence was kind and patient, especially with the children. When his uncle would get upset, Clarence would try to get him out of the house to protect Belle. Clarence was the only one who could calm Wilbert with funny stories and jokes.

Wilbert helped Clarence find a job at the Cadillac Company. Shortly after, though, Wilbert lost his. And as usual he took his frustration out on Belle, screaming while slapping and pushing her. Belle could no longer take this treatment; she was afraid for herself and her children. She finally divorced Wilbert in 1921. Granddaughter, I am surprised that she stayed with him that long.

Belle, her two girls, and Amelia came to visit us about that time. Clarence wanted to come to see me, too, but he had to work at the factory. To prepare, I made some of my chicken soup that the girls loved and a pie from our cherry tree. Ben met them at the train station that morning. I was so excited when I felt the train coming and went out on the front porch to watch for them. But I could see them all waving and smiling at me as they walked up the hill carrying their bundles. Ben had to stop and rest for a while, and he looked so frail.

◆◆◆◆◆◆◆ Ben's Passing ◆◆◆◆◆◆◆

By this time Ben was well into his nineties. He had lost most of his teeth. His gray hair had thinned out so you could see his scalp, his once-dark skin looked chalky, and his skin hung like a loose suit. Daniel and I had to feed and bathe Ben, although he would not eat much and he was tired all the time. Ben had a horrible cough, and towards the end, that cough just did not go away.

It must have been all that soot and ash in his lungs from his dirty job. I tried to care for my Ben, but I had problems breathing, so Daniel cared for him when I could not.

Ben knew that he was at the end of his Earth-walk, and he told me to send a message for Belle to come. The next day he thanked me for being with him and for giving him a family. He told me that he was going to see our passed children soon. Even though I was happy that he would be with our lost children, I also felt jealous, as the picture of my long-gone little ones came into mind.

Before Belle could arrive, Ben asked me to tell her that he was sorry that he could not live long enough to see her again and that he loved her. Then he turned to Daniel and told him that he had been a good son and an honest, good-hearted man. I kissed Ben good night and he passed in his sleep, not long after his 100th birthday. The next day Belle arrived to help with all the burial arrangements.

◆◆◆◆◆◆◆   The Telegram   ◆◆◆◆◆◆◆

She came to see me again two years later when she received a telegram which read: NEED YOU—COME HOME. LOVE, UNCLE DANIEL. Belle and the girls boarded the next train to Madeira. I could not meet them at the door as I had done so many times before. My swollen ankles could hardly hold me up and my eyesight was beginning to fail me. Instead Belle found me in bed, sick with bronchitis. Daniel thought that I was going to die.

Before Belle arrived, Daniel did all the cooking, cleaning, and gardening in addition to working his job. Now at least Belle could help him. You know, granddaughter, that although Daniel loved sleeping in the backyard in the warm months where he could watch the stars, he slept inside the house so he could hear me if I needed help.

I believe that I was able to recover, even if it was for only a little while, because of all the care I received from Daniel and Belle. She was such a good cook and I enjoyed all that she did for me. She reminded me of Maggie so much.

Watching Belle's daughters, Margaret and Violet, playing in the garden as Belle and I sat in the kitchen made it feel like the old days again. Belle even combed my hair, which had become thinner and gray, parting it down the middle and wrapping it into a bun. She helped me dress myself in my long black dress and pinned my broach that had Maggie's photograph high on my chest. Belle would also help me put on my straw hat when we sat outdoors. When she made meals, she wore my big apron.

I was worried about Daniel being alone, though, when I passed on. He was such a wonderful person, but he was shy around people outside the family, after all the teasing he took as a boy.

While Daniel was at work, I asked Belle what we could do about him when I was no longer here. We came up with the idea of asking Amelia and Clarence to move back home with him. That way they could be here for him, and Daniel could leave the house to them when he passed away.

Many businesses were letting people go from their jobs, and if things did not get better, it was only a matter of time until Clarence would be out of work, too. My little red brick shotgun house would become the family home. It would be a place where any of the family could come when they needed comfort.

One day when Belle was out in the garden with the girls, I saw some papers that she had left on the table. Starting to straighten them up, I realized that the one on top was a postcard with a picture of two open roses. When Belle came into the house, I told her that it was very pretty and asked who sent it to her. That is when she sat down and explained the postcard to me.

She said that she had bought the postcard for her mother. That surprised me because her mother was gone. Belle first read the address to me, and then continued with the greeting:

To: Mrs. Marg Stapleton

In Memory of My Mother (age 50, when she passed away).

Then Belle turned the card over and read:

Mother's Birthday, With Love
There's always a greeting ready for a sister,
Friend or brother.
But bore [strain] my brain as I will
It must come from the heart for Mother.
I love you, Mama.
Love, Belle

Granddaughter, as I watched Belle's lips, I knew that everything was going to be okay. It was okay for me to go. I knew that the love would continue, even when I was gone. Daniel would be okay. The grandchildren would be okay, and I could finally go to be with my mother after all these years. I felt that even though many things seemed to go wrong or not exactly the way I wanted them to go, it was all working out in the end. I had done what I could with what I had. I had given all of myself to my family.

My passing was not really an end but just another step on my pathway. As we hugged, I felt Belle's strength. She felt my pride.

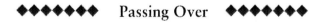 **Passing Over**

Granddaughter, as my days drew to an end, my mind wandered as I thought about the changes to come. I sat outside to think, resting in my favorite chair next to Ben's empty one. Daniel slept without a sound nearby. I watched the evening sky.

I could see the entire Heaven start to darken as the light slipped away. A paradise of glittering stars came into my sight, a magnificent splendor there before me only for the lifting of my eyes to see. I prayed to the Creator of Heaven and Earth that I would not observe without due appreciation and gratitude.

This glorious vista glided past my head, too many starry embers to calculate, see, or understand. I felt a soft cool breeze on my moist lips as it blew past. The darkness drew the sun's radiance from below the horizon. When the sun returned, it began to warm my cheeks.

I knew that with the passing of time, my existence would change. A day, an hour, and a moment would carry the *big change*, as it does for each of us. I wanted to be strong like Mother when I passed over.

Finally I drew in my last breath of sweet air. My eyes viewed their last image of my son in the garden by my home. My heart beat for the last time. I knew that motion, life, and sound continued around me, but I could no longer experience them. Everything was peaceful. There was a drawing away from familiar things of life—and a new beginning.

I laid every possession down. I was washed clean of all pain, fear, guilt, regrets, and grief. In a flitter of a humming bird's wing, the soft green flickering glow of a firefly, the wave of a hand, a step on a path, and the hoarse echo of a newborn's cry—change already came. A new mission began. The only thing unchanged—my love.

Maternal Lineage:
Belle Tiberghien Hall Kerske

1st Great - grandmother	Second Husband	Year Married	Children
Belle Tiberghien Hall (1887-1960)	Paul Kerske (aka Jim Mooney) (1894-1934)	1924	*Robert 1927-

*Adopted by Amelia and Clarence

Maternal Lineage:
Violet Hall Perin

Grandmother	Husband	Year Married	Children
Violet Tiberghien Hall (1914-2002)	Everet Perin (1907-1978)	1933	Violet Betty 1934- Peggy Ann 1935- James 1943-

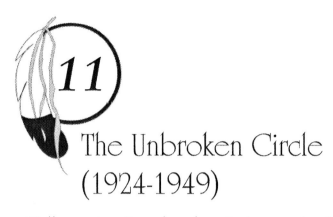

The Unbroken Circle (1924-1949)

Hello again, Grandmother. It is me, April, your great-great-great granddaughter. I am glad to see you in the cool, misty evening. You may not know that my mother, Violet Betty, is the first-born daughter of Belle's daughter Violet Hall. I want to tell you about my great-grandmother Belle and other family members who knew and loved you and passed after your passing. When I see you again in the Whispering Garden, I will tell you about my mom, my children, and grandchildren.

Something roused me tonight as I slept and I thought that I might come out to find you here in the garden. Thank you for being here for me. Your life stories draw me nearer to you and the people of your mother—the Monacans.

I also have some stories to share with you. Since your time on Earth, a great deal has changed. I would like to tell you mainly about Belle, Amelia, and Daniel, who lived until 1949.

Granddaughter I am very interested in what you have to say, so please continue.

Grandmother, before I share my story, I want you to know why I began searching for you. I have always loved you, and I have wondered and daydreamed about you as far back as I can remember. I always wanted to meet and talk with you. As a child, I even pretended that I was you sometimes.

I knew you through stories that my Grandma Violet, your great-granddaughter, used to tell me and from your photograph hanging on her dining room wall. How royal you look in your black dress with the big white collar and long, puffy sleeves. Your gold broach pinned to the neckline makes you look so beautiful. A bonnet, tied under your chin, covers your black hair with a few gray streaks, just like the silver night.

A few years before Grandma Violet passed, she gave me your photograph, which is now hanging in my home. While I was visiting Grandma, she asked me whether there was anything special of hers that I would like to have someday. I guess she knew her time on Earth was soon to end and she wanted to make sure that she left me something that I would value. Not saying a word, my eyes glanced toward your picture.

She smiled at me, laughing quietly, and said that she knew what my answer would be before she asked. Grandmother, she and I had a way of often reading each other's minds or maybe we just knew each other's heart.

She rose from her chair as I was leaving to walk me to the door, but on her way past the dinning-room table, she stopped to take down the big oval framed photo, placing it in my hands. I stood there speechless because I could not believe what she had just done. I wanted her to keep it awhile longer, but she said, 'No.'

She knew how to touch my heart. Grandma Violet said that she wanted to be sure that your picture would always be mine because she knew that I loved it more than anything else of hers. I had no idea that the photo would ever be mine. I thought it would go to one of her three children. My eyes burned and a warm salty taste came into my mouth. I tried to hold back, but the tears rolled down my face as she wrapped her arms around me.

I also have pictures of Maggie and Belle and eight

generations of our family, starting with you, in my baby book and in photo albums. When my husband and I moved to our new home, I took many of those photos out of the albums and started framing the photos and hanging them in my art room where I work.

Unlike Enyard, I use my gift to create. I paint in oils and acrylics on large canvas. Grandmother, I paint tropical birds and butterflies, which you probably could find in your plant and animal book. I also enjoy sewing, a talent I must have gotten from you.

◆◆◆◆◆◆◆ Your Special Day ◆◆◆◆◆◆◆

Grandmother, let me complete the circle and tell you what I know about the events after your passing. I will start my story where you left off with yours. When you started to feel a little better in the early part of 1924, Belle returned home to care for her children. But she returned for your burial. All the family was there when you passed, and Belle dressed you in your favorite dress with your broach at the neckline. It is the same dress that you wore for your photograph.

Grandma Violet told me that you looked like a high-cheeked, oval-faced, royal queen with a pretty new hanky in your hands. You were buried with your old, worn book of plants and animals that Doctor Galt gave you, the one you used on your journey to Ohio. Amelia pressed some of your favorite flowers and placed them inside the book. Several family members laid family pictures next to you. And at your side was a bouquet of Daniel's beautiful garden flowers.

Great-grandmother Belle told me that the entire family attended your burial in Evergreen Cemetery not far from your home. Amelia read a verse from the Bible. Belle also spoke, saying what was in everyone's heart. She described you as a wise, family-loving woman who envied no one. Treating everyone with kindness and respect, you required little for yourself but wanted to give your children the world. She also said that you knew the right words to help others, although you could not hear what they said.

Grandmother, I want you to know that Belle continued to praise you until her own death in 1960, at the age of 72. I was only eight, but she would tell me about you whenever we visited. Belle would tell the family that you were honorable, cheerful, and positive, even though she could often see your broken heart and losses behind your smile. She said that you held your head high. She also said that you were full of compassion, helping anyone in need, without thinking or wanting anything in return. You were her shining star and often eased the loneliness that Belle felt because she did not have her own mother. Grandmother, you were Belle's *Wechumpe*, the name that your own grandmother called your mother when she was a girl.

Belle had never seen so many beautiful flowers placed on top of one grave. Daniel had picked every flower out of the garden and placed them there. Violet and her older sister Margaret tied long purple and yellow silk ribbons on the tall bouquets of iris and gladiolas. Belle once showed me her Bible with the faded ribbon she had taken from the top of your grave a few days after the burial. She also showed me how she wrote all the family names and birth dates on the inside cover.

The family stayed a couple of days at your house after your burial, gathering in the flowerless garden or reminiscing around the kitchen table, telling old stories. Grandma Violet would tell me what she had said that day: She did not believe that you were really deaf because you knew everything she did. She said that you knew what she was doing wrong when you were in the other room and that you even knew what she was saying behind your back.

Violet's older sister, Margaret, would tell me that Violet wished you had lived to your 100th birthday like Grandpa Ben. And Belle said that she loved how you always wore your big plaid aprons with the big pockets so you could carry extra hankies around to clean the children whenever they came close to you. She said that you kept the family looking clean with hankies and spit, and for bigger jobs you just used the whole apron to scrub the children.

Amelia said that she loved looking at your face as you watched the little ones play. She said that she always thought that you could see more children playing in the garden. She thought that you still saw your Elizabeth, Mary, Albert, and the others. She loved sitting on your lap in your old chair when she lived with you while her mother was in the hospital.

Grandma Violet told me how Uncle Daniel would love sharing how you were such a loving daughter. He would tell the family how he heard you talking to your mother in your sleep during the days just before you passed. Grandma Violet would tell me that tears would fill his eyes when he said that he heard you say that you were sorry that you had lost the old ways and traditions and did not know how to find them—that they had been stolen from you.

After you passed away, Daniel sat in the house, looking at your big oval picture hanging on the wall. He promised your picture to Belle, but asked her not to take it for a while. She agreed, but in fact, she never took the picture until long after Daniel had passed away. Many years later, Belle passed it down to her daughter, Violet, my grandma.

◆◆◆◆◆◆◆ Great-Grandmother Belle's Happy Life ◆◆◆◆◆◆◆

Grandmother, you no longer have to worry about Belle because her second husband, Paul Kerske, turned out to be the love of her life, just as your Abner was to you.

Born in Germany, Paul moved to the United States with his family as a young boy and became a US citizen. Grandmother, two months before your passing, you, too, became a citizen because Congress passed a law saying that Indians born in the United States were now citizens. You were finally a citizen of your own country, and no one would ever take an Indian child away again to any boarding school.

Belle used to show us lots of photos of Paul in his Navy uniform. He joined the Navy when he was 25, before he met Belle. Seven years younger than Belle, Paul was a handsome man. He was 5 feet 5 inches and was in excellent shape because he had been a boxer in the Navy. He had dark brown eyes and medium brown hair.

Paul continued boxing after he married Belle, and he chose *Jim Mooney* as his boxing name. *Jim Mooney* was a famous author at the time, who respected Indians, and Paul wanted to show how much he admired that man.

From time to time, he and Belle would travel the country to boxing matches, while Amelia would watch the children. But after a year, he knew that he no longer had the energy to continue that sport, so he decided to train other boxers. He also promoted and advertised boxing matches.

Paul knew that he would be away from home more often and longer, so he asked Belle to come with him. Belle went everywhere with Paul, helping with the paperwork, running errands, and booking matches for the men he trained.

Because Belle knew that she would be away for long

periods of time, she asked Amelia to watch the girls. Amelia was thrilled to help her sister because Amelia had no children of her own. The girls loved Amelia like a second mother, and she was happy to have the girls stay with her. Soon Amelia and Clarence would take the girls and move in with Uncle Daniel in Madeira at your home, as you had wanted, Grandmother. Everyone wanted to care for Uncle Daniel, who was alone in the home you gave him.

◆◆◆◆◆◆◆ A Special Gift ◆◆◆◆◆◆◆

After Belle and Paul had been married for almost a year, Belle was pregnant again, but she was not showing yet. She and Paul returned to Madeira to see her girls and Amelia and Clarence. Amelia and Clarence had been married for nearly five years, with no children of their own, and they wanted children more than anything. Belle knew how patient and loving her sister was and how she needed a little one of her own. So Belle agreed to let Amelia adopt the baby. But Belle did not want her girls to know the truth, not when they were so young.

Amelia's adopting her sister's child was not a new idea for Amelia and Belle. About six years earlier when Belle was expecting, the sisters made a similar agreement. But that baby girl passed away two days after birth, and Amelia was still childless.

Belle, Paul, Amelia, and Clarence discussed what would be best for everyone. Belle was turning 40, times were hard, and she and Paul were on the road a lot. They all agreed that they would love and care for this child as one family, the way they did with the girls, but this baby would be raised as Amelia's own. Belle's girls would be told that the baby was their cousin, but Belle and Paul would send money to help with all the children.

A big and strong baby boy was born in 1927. Amelia named him Robert. It was the happiest day in Amelia's life. She was so excited when she first looked into the face of her own son. She loved being a mother. Her sister had given her the greatest gift she had ever received. It was the gift of life and love.

My Grandma Violet, then 12, came home from school the afternoon that the baby was born. She could smell sweet baked beans cooking in her aunt's big brown bean pot in the oven, as she ran in through the door to put her school things down before going out to play. She saw Amelia rocking in her chair, but this time she was not crocheting or looking through the new baseball book that Uncle Clarence bought for her.

This time her aunt was feeding and humming "Sleepy Little Baby," one of your favorite songs to a baby. My grandma could not understand why Amelia never told anyone that she was expecting. Grandma Violet was told that the baby was born that morning and it was bad manners to ask those questions and to say nothing like that again.

Violet said no more, but the questions were still there: *Why wasn't Aunt Mee Mee in bed? Why was she feeding the baby with a bottle instead of the way most of the other mothers fed their new babies? Why didn't my mother come to help with the baby? Mother always came when something important happened but not this time.*

Everyone was happy to have such a beautiful baby. Belle's daughters always wanted to take him for walks in the buggy or play with him. Sometimes the girls fussed at each other about who had more time with him. Belle visited as much as she could. She knew that she had done the right thing and was reassured every time she saw the family. The sisters both loved all the children dearly.

####### ◆◆◆◆◆◆◆ Hard Times ◆◆◆◆◆◆◆

Grandmother, the country continued to change, and the Great Depression Years started. People lost lots of money and their jobs. Banks and many businesses had to close. Some people even killed themselves. Times were hard for almost every family, and to take their minds off troubles, people were still interested in attending boxing events. Other people listened to the boxing matches on the radio at home and in the bars.

So Paul continued working and making money during the Great Depression. But after 10 years of marriage in 1934, Paul became ill, right after his new young boxer won a match in Kansas City. Paul passed at the Kansas City Veteran's Hospital. The doctor was surprised that Paul had not passed away earlier because Paul was a *blue baby*, meaning that his blood did not have enough oxygen in it. That is probably why he did not have a lot of energy at times. The doctor said that Paul faced a lot of risks to his heart when he was boxing.

After Paul's burial, Belle moved in with Amelia. Belle helped with the cleaning, cooking, laundry, and childcare. Amelia's son, who was eight, called his birth mother Aunt Belle.

Belle worked as a short-order cook in a small restaurant down the street to help with the income. Always happy, she had lots of friends in town, and everyone was glad to have her home and wanted to spent time with her. Grandmother, Belle finally got her wish about her hair. When she had a few extra dollars, she would go to a beauty shop where the owner would cut and curl Belle's hair.

Belle used little sayings like 'I am waiting for my ship to to come in, and a penny for your thoughts.' Belle and Amelia enjoyed being together. They both loved the Cincinnati Reds Baseball

Team and often attended games or listened to them on the radio. The two sisters did everything together.

◆◆◆◆◆◆◆ Beloved Daniel ◆◆◆◆◆◆◆

After your passing, Daniel worked at the Cedar Hills Dairy Farm, where you used to buy milk, continuing to work there until 1945. Daniel never wanted much of anything for himself, just like you, Grandmother. He continued enjoying the outdoors, sleeping under the stars. He was truly a Monacan because he worshipped nature. In the coldest part of winter, Amelia encouraged him to sleep in the basement where it was warmer. But he would prefer to sleep outside.

Daniel never married and never had any children. And everyone called him Uncle Daniel. He remained close to Amelia and Clarence and the rest of his family until passing. Dan was so loved. Your grandson Scott named his son after Daniel. And when Amelia's son, Robert, grew older, Daniel helped him get a summer job at the dairy. In return, Robert took Daniel to watch Robert play football games at school. Daniel continued to grow flowers, picking some every time he visited your grave.

Daniel bought a couple of different cars, which he loved to drive. He had a black 1935 convertible car that he rode around town. He also drove the family to his favorite fishing spot, where they would all picnic.

Grandmother, Daniel helped pass on your traditions and culture you taught him, so all was not lost. Daniel was Monacan through you, even though he also had some Algonquin, Delaware, and Shawnee blood from his father. Wanting all the family to know that they, too, had Indian blood, Daniel would give the children Indian-head nickels, just to let the children know who they really are. To this day, my mother, Betty, still loves those nickels. I believe that he would have written wonderful stories had he known how to write. But the White Man did not give him a chance.

When Daniel was in the last years, he started having problems with his lungs, and he had to quit working. With less than a year to live, Daniel went with his two nieces, Belle and Amelia, to Florida to visit their sister, Ida, and her husband, Alva, and his two daughters that Ida raised as her own. Daniel, age 81 at the time, looked forward to the trip, even though he had little strength left.

I have lots of photos of that trip. But the ones that show he is the happiest are photos of sitting on the docks, watching boats come into port. Daniel is just sitting there with the sun beating down on him. He told his nieces that the only thing that could have made his day any better was if he could have shared it with you.

No longer able to walk, Daniel passed away quietly at Ida's home, with family at his bedside. He did not open his eyes as he said his last words, but a single tear rolled down his cheek. 'I am going to see Mama again.' A warm May morning in 1949 changed the family's life forever because Uncle Daniel was no longer there. The girls cried because their Uncle Daniel was the sweetest, most gentle man that any of them had even known, but they knew that he was ready to leave.

They wanted to bury Daniel near you in Ohio, but they were unable to make the necessary arrangements, so they buried Daniel in Tampa, near Ida's home. Belle and Amelia saved two red roses from his grave that they took back to Ohio. One rose was placed in Belle's Bible and the other was given to you, the one who loved him most.

◆◆◆◆◆◆◆ Sam's Accident ◆◆◆◆◆◆◆

Grandmother, I would like to tell you what I learned about the accident that happened to Maggie's first husband, Sam. When their sons George and Charles were young men, they finally learned the truth about their father's accident.

The year was 1925, a year after you passed, when George read an article in The Cincinnati Times about Sam's best friend, Barney, who worked with Sam at the billposter office. George always thought that Barney knew what had happened to Sam, but Barney was afraid to say. Now he was nearly 70, and the boys needed to know.

George drove his brothers Charles and Scott to visit Barney, who was recuperating at Cincinnati Hospital. Barney told them that he never wanted to say anything before because he did not want to hurt Maggie.

The story passed down was that Barney told the boys that Sam was always worried about expenses, especially with so many children. Sam was looking for a way to make some money to help the family and he met a guy who had given him a couple of good gambling tips. Barney said that after winning a few times, Sam felt lucky and placed a sizable bet with a bookie. Sam trusted the bookie, thinking that another win could help with the bills and maybe even with a down payment on a house for Maggie and the kids.

But things went wrong for Sam and he lost lots of money. Sam told Barney that a man who worked with the bookie threatened Sam to come up with the money or Sam would learn a lesson. Grandmother, the man killed Sam and made it look like an accident—all because a good man wanted to help his family. Barney told George, Charles, and Scott to remember that their father loved them and died trying to make a better life for them.

The men shared the story with others in the family, especially proud of their father from that day on. Years later George passed on from a gas leak in his apartment and had had a military funeral. Scott moved out of state, losing touch with the rest of the family, and Charles passed away at 70, survived by his wife and son, Sonny.

◆◆◆◆◆◆◆ A Wish Fulfilled ◆◆◆◆◆◆◆

Grandmother, I want you to know that in September 2005, I visited the Monacan Indians in Virginia. I met Chief Kenneth Branham at a powwow held at Natural Bridge, our holy ground. I listened to the Muddy Creek Band and watched dancers. I also met Vicky, who is another Penn descendant.

Grandmother, I am fulfilling your wish by searching our roots. No longer do you need to worry about losing our Indian language, traditions, customs, and culture. I have applied for tribal membership and am waiting for an answer from the Monacan Indians.

I found records proving the connections of each generation of our family. I spent years collecting what the White Man took away in such a short time. You may rest more easily now because our circle is not broken. One hundred forty-three years have past, and seven more generations have been born, but a spark in my *red* heart stayed alive to find home, listen to beating drums, and look out at the beautiful Blue Ridge Mountains.

I spoke your name into the wind, as I stood there in absolute peace. I am hoping for acceptance as a tribal member, but whatever happens, my search for you and our people has been worthwhile.

Growing Stronger

Beyond the horizon,
a distant cry shatters the deep cold silence.
Thunder rumbles and lightning flashes through the sapphire night.
A spirit soars high above the tallest trees
in exploration.
The last specks of daylight disappear on the western horizon.
Billows of clouds whirl across a
darkening cobalt sky.
A powerful wind lashes past.
A blazing fire sizzles. A woman quickly opens her eyes
to see the eyes of the bear.
Far—far away
another lonely voice calls out.
White steamy breath
pours out from her mouth.
The azure mountain brook
continues to charge over slippery rocks on its way to the river.
A panting doe stops to drink.
And the bright yellow moon
stares down, surrounded by shimmering morning stars.
Another day has slipped into yesterday.
A white dove coos.
A new generation is born,
as much a part of the Earth
as the small creatures and insects,
as the landscapes and water,
as the plants and birds,
as the buffalo, wolf, and bear,
as of all life.

To You, Grandma Violet

I think of you, Grandma, every day, as I miss you. I take time to try to feel your presence, see your smile, and hear your voice. You are strong in my heart. In dreams I have seen you many times. I find myself step outside in the misty silence of the night. A violet colored breeze is swirling and blowing softly. I smell your perfume. I walk from a dark place onto a silvery carpet of moonlight to find you. You are there smiling and waiting for me. I go to you and put my head on your shoulder and my arms around you. I tell you that I love and miss you, and you hold me again, telling me wonderful family stories, just as when I was a young girl.

A healing ache comes over me and I take a deep breath. You are part of my very soul. I will never forget all the times that we shared. I will never give up. I will never forget where I come from and I will never—never let you go. Thank you for being so good to me. Some day I will share stories with you. *Lapich Knewe—Lu Peach U Now Away.* I will see you again. I will see you again in the Whispering Garden.

Author's Notes:
Connecting Past, Present, and Future

The spirits of my ancestors have helped me connect with my rich heritage. Knowing their story has revealed to me the importance of leaving a legacy for future generations. I am compelled to share my ancestors' stories as a way to connect the past with the present and future.

An adventurous part of me enjoys distant morning thunder. I love feeling the early cool misty air, seeing the moonlit sky, and watching the sun unhurriedly rise at daybreak. I am filled with wonder when a flower blooms, a chick hatches, or a butterfly emerges from its cocoon. Like the butterfly, I too, have had to shed my cocoon to start a new life.

I feel at peace when I'm closest to nature. During nights alone outdoors, I feel connected to Mother Earth. Some of my most relaxing times have been spent under trees watching the stars, on mountains, and in water.

My favorite place to visit is Dry Falls near Franklin, North Carolina. The falls received their name because there is an empty space, or cavern, behind the flowing waters. I have a similar space in me that was worn away by the harshness of my young adult life. It's a place that I can go, not to remember, but look out from. The edges are covered over with delicate mosses, thus smoothing the shapes to hide the disfigured damage.

I also feel connected to the many generations of women in my family—not just because of a genealogy; it is much more powerful and lasting. This burning need to reconnect has compelled me to share with you my ancestors' lives, loves, losses, pain, and glory.

I learned much about my heritage from stories passed down from one generation to the next, one link connecting to the next. Personal letters, cards, and photos helped me unfold the saga of my heritage. What I did not learn from my family, I uncovered by researching census records, birth and death certificates, and maps. Hours—stretching into years—were spent in museums, libraries, historical archives, historical societies, and on the Internet. Finally, my own thoughts, imagination, and even my dreams have helped me fill in the blanks.

I also have traveled the length of the United States from the southern tip of the Florida Keys to Canada. And I stood in awe of such majestic sights as Niagara Falls, the Great Smokey Mountains, and Natural Bridge.

◆◆◆◆◆◆◆ My Special Place ◆◆◆◆◆◆◆

When I cannot go to the mountains or woods to relax, I have a quiet room in my home where I can shut out today's world. The past connects with the present in this room. Maybe that's why this room is special. Early morning sun creeps in from my east window to toss light through hanging crystals that produce rainbows of spinning dancing colors. I can feel at ease, read, paint, or meditate.

Lavender walls hold my art. Pictures of loved ones reflect rays of light into my soul. My Grandma Violet's end table has three small drawers holding precious memories. A pair of her socks, a bookmark, a violet washcloth, a hanky, a dried yellowish rose, and a necklace of fake pearls—all sit inside. I pull out her sweater to smell and place against my cheek. I keep a personal note in one drawer that she left for me. The envelope says 'For April when I pass away.'

A large wooden art easel sits in one corner, having witnessed over 200 paintings I have done in the past few years. A horseshoe found during a long walk through the forest hangs on one corner. An Indian corn doll with no eyes stands next to Indian dolls from my mom and grandmother. Two lanterns, each from a different grandfather, sit alongside an old crystal radio. Candles, music boxes, an old Raggedy Andy Doll, and family antiques fill the room. A large wooden cabinet with shelves and chicken mesh doors is decorated with sheer curtains and sits against the wall holding family memories and albums—photos that have come alive for me.

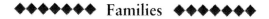 Families

I often think about love and the connection of families. These connections can be fluid like water, strong like a storm, big like the sky, and alive like Mother Earth. I cannot see love, but I can see the results of it or lack of it. I can feel it inside of me. Love from my mother, grandmother, aunts, and other family members has been with me all my life. Like a circle, my ancestors, my mom, my children, grandchildren, and I are bound by unbreakable bonds.

Descendants of
Mary Jane Boatwright

April's Grandmothers	Husband	Year Married	Children, Born-Died (Years)	
Mary Jane Boatwright Great-great-great-great grandmother	William Penn	1837	Mary Ann	1838-1924 (86)
Mary Ann Great-great-great- grandmother	1st husband: Abner Cox	1865	Maggie	1863-1913 (50)
			Daniel	1867-1949 (82)
			Elizabeth	1870-1870 (0)
	2nd husband: Benjamin Holmes	1875	Mary	1876-1886 (10)
			Albert	1878-1882 (4)
Maggie Great-great grandmother	1st husband: Sam H. Tiberghien	1880	Sammy Jr.	1881-1883 (2)
			William	1883-1918 (35)
			Ida	1885-1961 (76)
			Twins	1886-1886 (0)
			Belle	1887-1960 (73)
			George	1888-1959 (71)
			Charles	1889-1959 (70)
			Willard	1890-unknown
			Twins	1891-1891 (0)
			Amelia	1893-1982 (89)
			Mary	1894-1897 (3)
			Bertha	1895-1897 (2)

Descendants of
Mary Jane Boatwright (continued)

April's Grandmothers	Husband	Year Married	Children, Born-Died (Years)		
Maggie Great-great grandmother	2nd husband: Enyard Stapleton	1898	Scott	1899-1964	(65)
			James	1901-1922	(21)
			Mary	1902-1904	(2)
			Twins	1904-1904	(0)
Belle Great grandmother	1st husband: Wilbert Hall	1910	Margaret	1911-1992	(81)
			Violet	1914-2002	(88)
			Baby Son	1915-1915	(0)
			Baby Son	1919-1919	(0)
	2nd husband: Paul Kerske (aka Jim Mooney)	1924	Robert	1927-	
Violet Grandmother	Everet Perin	1933	Violet Betty	1934-	
			Peggy Ann	1935-	
			James	1943-	
Betty Mother	Clifford Clark	1950	Violet April	1952-	
			Clifford Jr.	1954-	

Descendants of
Mary Jane Boatwright (continued)

April's Grandmothers	Husband	Year Married	Children, Born-Died (Years)
April (Shaya)	Richard Ebersole		Darren* 1969-
			Brandi Jean* 1972-
			Violet Betty 1978- Eve*
April's Grandchildren	Travis Dean 1990		*From previous marriages
	Tricia Leigh 1991		
	Tiffany Ada 1993		
	Kyleigh Belle 1998		
	Gabrielle Violet 1999		

Family Information

Mary Jane Boatwright

The 1830 census for Lynchburg, Campbell County, Virginia, indicates that Mary Jane is the head of her family, living alone. She is between 20 and 30 years old.

William Penn

The 1850 census taken in Fauquier County, Virginia, indicates that William, a Mulatto male, is the head of the house. He lives with his 12-year-old daughter Mary Ann; Ellen, who is 38, and her children: (1) 13-year-old Arthur; (2) nine-year-old Elya; (3) eight-year-old Delaware; (4) six-year-old Susan; and (5) four-year-old Sarah; Willie, who is 28, and her children: (1) four-year-old Simeon and (2) one-year-old Scott. The women and their children are listed as Negro. Their state of birth is Virginia, William Penn's occupation is stonemason, and the value of the home is $150. One of their neighbors, 50-year-old Ann Thompson, lives with her grown son and daughter in a home valued at $800. Another neighbor is Dudley Smith, a merchant, living alone in a home valued at $100. Other neighbors are farmers, laborers and one wheelwright.

Mary Ann Penn

The 1860 census for Williamsburg, Virginia, indicates that Mary Ann is an insane patient of the Eastern Lunatic Asylum, whose approximate age is 26, but she is actually 22.

Mary Ann Penn Cox

The 1870 census for Cincinnati, Hamilton County, Ohio, indicates that 32-year-old Abner Cox is head of the house. He is a carpenter, who owns a home valued at $150. His wife is Mary Ann, age 31. Their children are Margaret (Maggie) ages seven, Daniel, age two, and Elizabeth, age three months.

Three pieces of information from the census are incorrect: (1) That the family is White, (2) That they were born in Ohio, and (3) That their parents were also born in Ohio. The correct information is that the family is Indian, and Mary and her parents were born in Virginia.

Mary Ann Penn Cox Holmes

The 1880 census for Cincinnati, Hamilton County, Ohio, indicates that Mary Ann lives with her husband Benjamin Holmes, a boiler cleaner, and four children on Hunt Street. They are all listed as Mulatto. Ben, 57, is a boilermaker from Mississippi. Seventeen-year-old Maggie works as a servant; Daniel, 12, is home with Mary, four; and Albert, two.

Mary Ann Penn Cox Holmes

The 1910 census for Cincinnati, Hamilton County, Ohio, indicates that Mary, 71, and Ben, 87, live on Miami Ave. Their son Daniel, 42, is single and works at the electric plant. Daniel's father was born in Ohio and his mother, in Virginia. The census states that Mary Ann has been married 37 years and only two of her five children are living at the time. Mary Ann and her husband own their own home, without any debts.

Mary Ann Penn Cox Holmes

The 1920 census for Cincinnati, Hamilton County, Ohio,

indicates that Mary Ann, 81, and Ben, 98, live with their only living son, Daniel Cox, 52. He works as a gardener.

Mary Ann Penn Cox Holmes

The 1924 death certificate for Mary Holmes states that her birth date is December 5, 1838. She lived 85 years, seven months, and 22 days, her date of death being August 1, 1924. The cause of death is chronic bronchitis, and she is buried in Miamiville, Ohio. Cemetery records indicate that Mary Holmes is buried in Section 1, but the exact location of the grave is unknown.

Maggie Cox Tiberghien Stapleton

The 1913 death certificate indicates that Maggie died in Longview Mental Hospital. Her cause of death is dementia paralytics (brain infection). She is buried in Spring Grove Cemetery.

Scott Stapleton and James Stapleton

The 1910 census of Cincinnati, Ohio, from the Cincinnati House of Refuge indicates that Scott, 11, and James Stapleton, 9, are *Inmates*.

Margaret Belle Tiberghien Hall

The 1920 census for Detroit, Michigan, indicates that Margaret Belle Hall, 32, is the wife of 34-year-old Wilbert Hall, who is listed as the head of the home. Their children are Margaret, 8, and Violet, 5. Also living in the home are Belle's sister, Amelia 26, and Wilbert's nephew, Clarence, 24

Margaret Belle Tiberghien Hall

The 1921 divorce decree from Wayne County, Detroit, Michigan, indicates that Wilbert Hall is guilty of several acts of extreme and repeated cruelty. His wife, Belle, is given custody of the two daughters, and he is ordered to pay $12 per week until the girls are 14. Wilbert Hall is ordered to give Belle $1, and she releases all rights, including dower rights, in any real estate that he owns or will acquire.

Margaret Belle Tiberghien Hall Mooney

The 1930 census for Cincinnati, Hamilton County, Ohio, indicates that Belle Mooney is living with her husband Paul Kerske, who goes by his boxing name, James Mooney, for the census report.

Maggie's Children

Nine of Maggie's 19 children lived to be adults, but the others lived to only age 3 or less. Early childhood deaths during Maggie's life were commonly caused by tuberculosis, diarrhea, dysentery, typhoid and scarlet fevers, diphtheria, and pneumonia.

Jimmy Stapleton

On August 11, 1922 Jimmy, Maggie's youngest son, fell off a train just before his 21st birthday. He died on the railroad tracks after losing both legs. His body was sent back to Cincinnati from Kansas City, Missouri. He is buried at Spring Grove Cemetery.

George Tiberghien

George joined the army during World War I. Years later he died in his sleep from a gas leak in his apartment.

Scott Stapleton

Scott built ships in the New York Harbor for the Navy. He later moved to Vermont.

Charles Tiberghien

Charles is buried in Madisonville Cemetery. His son, Sonny, lives in Hamilton, Ohio.

William Tiberghien

William married and had two daughters, Matilda and Loretta, who converted to Catholicism. The women ran a bakery in Cincinnati, Ohio, which their father helped them to start.

Ida Tiberghien Carpenter

Ida's husband, Alva Carpenter, worked at a concrete factory in Tampa, Florida. Ida and Alva had two children. She and her husband also raised chickens and planted fruit trees.

Amelia Tiberghien Wick

Amelia and her husband, Clarence, moved to Florida to run a motel after their son married. Extremely nearsighted, Amelia began wearing thick corrective lenses later in life. After Clarence passed, she moved in with her niece, Violet.

Willard Tiberghien

No information has been found to indicate what happened to Willard after childhood.

Belle Tiberghien Hall Kerske (Mooney)

Belle moved to Florida to live her last few years with her daughter, Violet.

DNA Testing:
Origin of Maternal Bloodline

Readers who are interested in determining their maternal bloodline might find the following information helpful:

• Trace Genetics, Inc., 4655 Meade Street, Suite 300, Richmond, CA 94804, tests for maternal bloodline and does other genetic testing. The test to trace maternal bloodline is the World-wide MT-DNA Test, which costs $200 and takes at least four weeks for the results. A box comes in the mail with a simple form that you complete. Swabs are provided for rubbing the inside of your cheek for 30 seconds. You need to wait for the swabs to dry before placing them in a special collection envelope. Thirty major maternal lineages are identified, but the test does not provide the percentages or specific geographic information like other tests.

• A Native-American MT-DNA Upgrade Test is also available. Of the 30 lineages, five (A, B, C, D, & X) are Native American. There is also a possibility of identifying an individual with a tribal match. Company technicians can run a sequence through the Native-American database to see whether they can match the information, but there's no guarantee that your match will be found.

• Trace Genetics, Inc., also offers a test to determine paternal bloodlines for five generations.

For more information, search the Internet by keying in words such as DNA testing, chromosome, genetics, and electropherogram.

DNA Testing:
My DNA Testing

The test was easy, but the waiting was hard. I submitted my swabs November 7, 2005. Finally results arrived.

I belong to the Eurasian Group H. H indicates my lineage, which came from Europe and East Asia as much as 20,000 years ago. One of my ancestral grandmothers was a European-Asian woman and my line traced back through her. Approximately 20 percent of European sequences are from Group H. If I belong to Group A ,B, C, D, or X, I could know from which tribe I am descended.

Through my extensive research of census, archives, family stories, and other means, I know my family lineage with much detail back at least to my 3rd great grandmother, Mary Ann Penn. Census records show that she was called White, Mulatto, and in some years Negro, a widely-used practice to wipe out the existence of people known as the American Indians.

Receiving the results of the first test prompted me to take another one in order to determine the percentages of European, Native American, Sub-Saharan African, and Asian ancestry. That test was taken the end of December 2005. On February 4, 2006, I found out the following percentages:

- 80 percent European
- 12 percent Asian-Native American
- 8 percent African

I also found out that Native Americans can show up as Asians because the ancestors of Native Americans migrated from Asia to what is now America.

Indian Tribal Membership

Armed with historical records and genetic information, I applied to become a member of the Monacan Nation on December 16, 2005.

The Monacans have a rigorous application registration procedure. Applicants must:

• Complete an application form, showing ancestral lines. An original birth certificate, social security number, and photo must be included.

• Prove ancestral connection to a Monacan tribal member (on the original membership rolls) through official census records, birth and marriage certificates, and other documents.

After the Monacan Council reviews all the information, applicants receive a letter of acceptance or denial. If the council approves, membership is sanctioned, with all privileges stated. Spouses may receive an honorary identification card, but they cannot vote in tribal elections. Charges for the application are very minimal.

My waiting starts again.

Tribal Division of the Sioux Nation Monacan Division Confederacies

Monacan Confederacy: Five Tribes
Monacan
Meiponsky
Mahoc
Nunaneuck or Nuntaly
Mohetan

Tutelo Confederacy: Three Tribes
Tutelo
Saponi
Occanichi

Manahoac Confederacy: Eight Tribes
Hassinnungaes
Mannahoac
Ontponeas
Stegarake
Shakakoni
Tauxitania
Tegninateos
Whonkenteas

History of Early Madeira

In earlier days Madeira was home to many Indians. But the area changed once the White Man moved in.

Farmers killed many wild animals and cut down numerous trees. Wolves and panthers, for example, were terrorizing the farmers. And hungry deer and rabbits had eaten the spring crops.

New roads were built. And as early as 1824, Montgomery Road made the trip to downtown Cincinnati easier. In 1857 the old Indian track crossing through Madeira was turned into Camargo Road, where tolls were collected from people passing through.

Changes came quickly, especially with the Civil War. Morgan's Raiders, the Confederate troops led by John Morgan raided Madeira for horses and food and foraged for other supplies.

The town started growing after the war. Advertisements painted a picture of perfection.

• Madeira residents were secure from epidemics like cholera and scarlet fever because of the high altitude of 320 feet.

• Building materials and coal were easily obtainable.

• Living conditions were affordable, and two-story homes had attractive lawns, apple and pear trees, grape vines, and stables and barns.

• There were many meadows, groves, and orchards, with row after row of plums and cherries.

• Other towns, such as Madisonville, Montgomery, Miamiville, and Plainville were nearby.

• Two traditional and well-respected societies, the Lyceum and the Odd Fellow's Club held regular meetings.

• The M & C Railroad, opened in 1866, ran east and west through town.

References

Books

Barbour, Philip, *Pocahontas and Her World*, Houghton Mifflin Company, Boston, 1970.

Garfield, Patricia, Ph.D., *Creative Dreaming: Plan and Control Your Dreams To Develop Creativity, Overcome Fears, Solve Problems, and Create a Better Self*, Amazon Books, New York, Second Edition, 1995.

---------*Healing Power of Dreams: Techniques for Interpreting and Using Your Dreams To Reveal Hidden Health Problems, Speed Your Recovery, and Promote Lifelong Health*, Simon & Schuster, New York, London, Toronto, Sydney, Tokyo, and Singapore, 1991.

Houck, Peter, W., MD, *Indian Island in Amherst County, Virginia*, Warwick House Publishers, Waynesboro, 1993.

Zwelling, Shomer, *Quest for a Cure: The Public Hospital in Williamsburg, Virginia*, 1773-1885, Colonial Williamsburg Foundation, Williamsburg, 2003.

Handwritten Documents

"The Eastern State Hospital Minutes, 1855-1866."
"The Eastern State Hospital Patient Records, 1859-1861."
Census Reports: 1830, 1850, 1860, 1870, 1880, 1910, 1920, 1930.
Death Certificates: Mary Holmes 1924, Margaret Stapleton 1913, James Stapleton 1922.
Divorce Certificate: Belle and Wilbert Hall 1921.

References (continued)

Newspapers and Magazines

Monacan News, Madison Heights, Virginia, 2005-2006.
Jones, Granville Lillard, "The History of the Founding of the Eastern State Hospital of Virginia," Reprinted From American Journal of Psychiatry, Volume 110, No. 9, Williamsburg, 1954.
Weiss, Michael, J., "Dare To Dream," Reader's Digest, February 2006, page 93-99.

Internet

Garfield, Patricia, Ph.D., February 2006,
http://www.patriciagarfield.com
Monacan Nation, *http://www.monacannation.com*
Wood, Karenne, Director, Historical Research, Monacan Nation, the Monacan Indians of Virginia, February 2006,
http://www.manataka.org/page470.html

A History Through Pictures

The home of Mary Ann Penn - 1850

In 1860 the hospital was called the Eastern Lunatic Asylum.

The hospital's
restriction chair

Margaret "Maggie"
(daughter to Mary Ann) - 1888

Maggie's
daughters,

Margaret
"Belle"
(left)
and
Mary
"Amelia"
(right)

Belle's daughter Violet
- 1914

Violet, age 3 with big sister
Margaret - 1917

Belle with her teenage
daughters - 1929

Violet's daughter
Violet "Betty" - 1934

Betty with her dog, Buddy
- 1935

Family outing in Uncle Dan's car - 1935

Family gathering at old Madeira home
of Mary Ann. Uncle Dan pictured at far left - 1937

Belle and Uncle Dan
on Tampa Beach - 1949

Betty with her daughter Violet "April"
at Baptism - 1952

Copy of death certificate for Mary Ann Penn

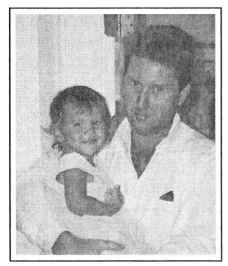

April's son Darren with April's
granddaughter Gabrielle

April's daughter Brandi
and family

April's daughter
Violet Eve

April's granddaughter
Gabrielle

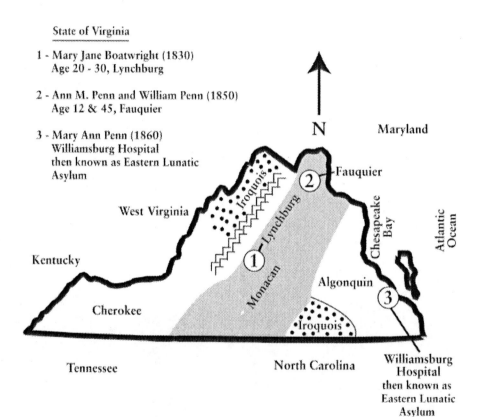

State of Virginia

1 - Mary Jane Boatwright (1830)
  Age 20 - 30, Lynchburg

2 - Ann M. Penn and William Penn (1850)
  Age 12 & 45, Fauquier

3 - Mary Ann Penn (1860)
  Williamsburg Hospital
  then known as Eastern Lunatic
  Asylum

N

Maryland

West Virginia

Iroquois

Lynchburg

Fauquier

Chesapeake Bay

Atlantic Ocean

Kentucky

① Monacan

Algonquin

③

Cherokee

Iroquois

Williamsburg Hospital then known as Eastern Lunatic Asylum

Tennessee

North Carolina

About the Author

Violet April (Shaya) Ebersole, descended from the Monacan Indians, enjoys searching through archives and historical information to learn more about her lineage. Her research has taken her to such places as Natural Bridge, the holy ground of the Monacans, and Lynchburg and Williamsburg, Virginia; two childhood homes of her great-great-great grandmother, Mary Ann Penn.

But April also enjoys staying at home with her husband, Richard, and spending as much time as possible with their children and grandchildren. She loves tending to her tropical garden, watching wildlife, and paddling through Florida waters in her tandem kayak. A talented artist, April has painted over 200 oils and acrylics. She also composes poetry.

April enjoys helping those in need. She has provided transportation for cancer patients for the past several years. And in the 1990s she worked with families of the deaf. She especially took pleasure in helping parents learn to communicate with their deaf children.

In 1991 an elderly Indian who met April at her church, where she would sign for deaf parishioners, called her Shayaholta Monticoma, meaning one who helps those in need. April likes to be called Shaya.

Ancestral Spirits Awaken Me is April's first full-length family saga, covering nine generations of strong, honest women, who have strived to keep their families intact in the face of adversity. April looks forward to sharing additional stories.

Printed in the United States
49749LVS00004B/160-510